Northfield
Past & Present

JOHN & JEAN SMITH

SUTTON PUBLISHING

Sutton Publishing Limited
Phoenix Mill · Thrupp · Stroud
Gloucestershire · GL5 2BU

First published 2001

Title page photograph: An aerial shot of
Trescott School and surrounding estate
encircled by Borrowdale Road and
Norrington Road. (*Trescott School*)

British Library Cataloguing in Publication Data
A catalogue record for this book is available from the
British Library.

ISBN 0-7509-

Typeset in 10.5/13.5 Photina.
Typesetting and origination by
Sutton Publishing Limited.
Printed and bound in England by
J.H. Haynes & Co. Ltd, Sparkford.

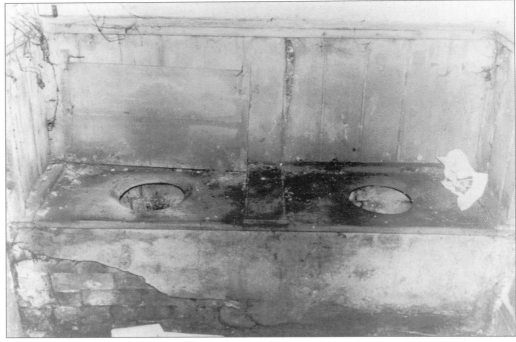

Two-seater privy at Hole Farm. What more is there to say about this cosy scene! (*Birmingham Central Library*)

CONTENTS

Greetings from Northfield! (*T. Hill*)

ACKNOWLEDGEMENTS

We would like to express our very grateful thanks to Birmingham Central Library's Archive and Local Studies sections; to the staff of Northfield Library who have all been most patient and helpful in assisting us to collect information; to the *Bromsgrove Messenger* who allowed us to use material and photographs from past articles in their papers, and to the many people of Northfield and surrounding districts who have welcomed us into their homes to relate memories and information and offered us the loan of their precious personal photographs. Special thanks must go to Mrs Olive Williams, Miss Patricia Tidey-Hamilton and Mrs Patricia Finney who gave us access to their projects on Northfield; Mr Tom Hill who provided much information and allowed us to use copies of his very extensive postcard collection, Mr Roger de Boer, who gave us access to his vast photographic collection of Northfield and provided much information for the text, and also to The Convent of our Lady of Charity, Mr I. Hamel-Cooke, Mrs B. Davis, Dr E.D. Graham, Mr P. Harding, Mrs D.I. Laugharne, Mr R.C. Saunders, Mrs M. Scott, Mr J. Stormont, Mrs J. Upton, Mrs M. Valente, Mr J. Withey and Northfield YMCA, all of whom wrote letters or lent us brochures and pamphlets from which we have drawn relevant details.

BIBLIOGRAPHY

Price, Victor J., *Birmingham Cinemas* – First published in 1986 by Brewin Books, Studley, Warwickshire. Reprinted 1988. New Edition 1995.
Occasional papers issued by Northfield Conservation Group.

A brewer's dray at the Black Horse Hotel in 1981. In the mid-1920s Mr Baron Davenport (controlling head of John Davenport and Sons) felt the existing Black Horse Hotel was too small to cope with the growing needs of the neighbourhood and the ever-increasing number of road users. With the advice of the architect Francis Goldsbrough of Bateman and Bateman, he decided to build a new, half-timbered Inn in the Neo-Tudor style of a country Baronial Hall, with its gabled bays and gravelled forecourt, giving a pleasant vision of 'Merrie England'. At first it was planned to have a formal garden of beds and paths, with three pavilions at the rear, but in 1930 this idea was abandoned and a bowling green and refreshment room, serving tea and beer, were installed. The new Black Horse was opened on 19 December 1929, and Miss Margaret Bondfield, one time Minister of Labour, wrote in the Visitors' Book: 'This is one of the most beautiful houses I have ever seen'. (*R. de Boer*)

INTRODUCTION

There is little evidence of Roman occupation in Northfield and no records exist of a settlement or population at that time. Approximately forty years after the Romans withdrew in 410 AD the Anglo Saxons invaded England, dividing the country into kingdoms as they advanced. Northfield, being one of the last areas to be conquered, was in the Kingdom of Mercia. About 300 years later the Danes invaded, but although they conquered Mercia in 874 AD again no evidence remains of a permanent settlement. Prior to this, in the early 800s Egbert created a united England by bringing each individual kingdom under one rule. Christianity was growing in many parts of the country and by uniting all the churches Egbert also formed one church. The dioceses were divided into parishes, each of which had a church and a priest. Apparently the feudal system was in existence as the local Lord of the Manor governed each parish.

Northfield, originally called Nordfeld, the name derived from a 'clearing' or feld in the north of the Forest of Feckenham, was mentioned in the Domesday survey of 1086 which states that Northfield had 33 inhabitants, including a priest, (by then a sign of extreme importance), and was worth 100 shillings, five times the value of Birmingham, which was assessed at 20 shillings. Also it owned nine ploughs against Birmingham's four, ploughs being a symbol of status at that time. It was originally part of Worcestershire and from Norman times developed into a small scattered village. In the thirteenth century, in addition to the chief Manor of Northfield and Weoley, the parish also included the sub-manors of Selly and Middleton, which correspond roughly to the modern districts of Northfield, Weoley Castle, Bartley Green, California, Selly Oak, Bournbrook, Selly Park and Bournville. A survey taken following the death of the Lord of the Manor in 1291, states that there were two water mills, and 80 ratepayers paying a total of £23 2s 6d. Several 'Jews' are also recorded but no indication given as to their occupations. It is at this time that we find Weoley Castle mentioned as the Lord's residence.

From 1315 to 1327 great suffering was caused by a series of famines. Owing to excessive rain, which prevented the crop from ripening, the price of corn rose to ten times its normal value. Many people died of starvation and cattle died from plague. Robbers roamed the countryside killing many people. Carrion became food in the fight for existence. It was feared children would be stolen and eaten, cannibalism in the gaols being not unknown. In 1349 Bubonic Plague arrived, sweeping the country, and people in their poor physical condition had little resistance.

By 1352 there were only 25 ratepayers in Northfield, the total amount paid being £1 13s 11d. No 'Jews' were mentioned in this Survey, they had apparently all been banished.

Under the feudal system all land was owned by the reigning monarch, but was distributed among his noblemen, who managed it for him. The people living on these lands were under the jurisdiction of the Lord of the Manor, and it was to him that all rents were due which, in the early days of Manorial Rule, were paid by means of Service; but in surveys in the fourteenth century seemed to be in the form of spices, particularly pepper and cinnamon, showing that Northfield traded with the outside world.

The life of the village was bound up with that of the Manor. The Manorial Court, held twice a year, dealt with all lawlessness, registered births and deaths, and ensured ditches were kept clear and roads and bridges repaired. Various officers (both male and female) were also appointed by the Court (the term of office being compulsory for one year) but these were unpaid and, in the main, unpopular. The appointments were a Reave, Bailiff, Tithing Men, Beer Tasters, Constable, Beadle and a Rent Collector. There were normally two Beer Tasters, but in 1457 eight are recorded, owing to the many complaints about the quality of the beer! Illicit brewing was frowned upon, the fine, if caught, being two pence.

The Somery family held the Manor of Northfield in the thirteenth century, but early in the following century, with the marriage of Joan de Somery, it passed to the Bettetourts. The Berkleys owned it in 1386 and retained possession until the sixteenth century when, in the reign of Henry VIII, Richard Jervoys bought it for £800. In the first half of the nineteenth century the Ledsam family bought it and it remained in their hands until 1902.

For some 800 years prior to 1840 Northfield covered approximately six miles across and four miles in length, consisting of about 5,800 acres. Sixteen acres were covered by water and about 4,000 acres were under cultivation. Mr Ledsam owned about 950 acres of parkland and the largest farm in the district was Middleton Hall farming approximately 230 acres. The average population was about four persons to one house and one house to about 20 acres, and before the mid-eighteenth century the Northfield population appears not to have exceeded 800. In 1563 records show 35 families, which had increased to 200 by 1776, and at the 1851 census the population was 2,460. A century later it had risen to approximately 73,000.

From 1898 until 1911 the parish was part of the Urban District of Kings Norton and Northfield, and in 1911, apart from a very small area at its north-west tip, which was added to Lapal parish, it became a suburb of Birmingham.

Since the beginning of the twentieth century immense changes have occurred in Northfield, changing it from a sleepy little village into a thriving area of roads, shops, schools, small industries, factories, and thousands of homes; and yet if one gazes across from the lych gate of the parish church to the Great Stone Inn the scene is much as it would have been 500 years ago.

1

Buildings & People

This building in the grounds of The Davids was known as
The Belvedere. The four cannon are believed to have been
used in the Indian Wars of 1807–8, after the Marquis of
Wellesley (1760–1842), who was the Governor of India
from 1797–1805, and may be regarded as the organiser of
the Indian empire. (*Sir Adrian Cadbury*)

In 1881 Thomas Hart, a cement manufacturer employing twenty men and two boys lived at The Davids with his wife, two sons, one daughter and two domestic servants. After Mr Laurence J. Cadbury bought and moved into The Davids following his marriage to Joyce he added two wings at a later date. He also created the garden and planted most of the trees surrounding it. From The Davids there was a track to the back of the convent at the end of which Shewards had a work shed. The ivy was removed in the early 1960s. Margaret Bearman recalls her father, Reg Lane being Treasurer of the Kings Norton & Northfield United Nations Association, of which Mrs Joyce Cadbury was President. They enjoyed many AGM's and suppers at The Davids. (*Sir Adrian Cadbury*)

The large house is where The Davids stood. Following the death of Mrs Joyce Cadbury in 1988 vandals caused extensive damage by setting fire to the house. Shortly afterwards the land was bought by Wimpy Homes who, together with Berkeley Homes, developed the site known as 'The Davids' and 'Bournville Copse' by building 12 five-bedroom, and 55 four-bedroom houses. (*J. Smith*)

A fine collection of mounted big game trophies brought back from Alaska, North America and East Africa in 1913 and 1934 by Mr Laurence Cadbury seen here in the games room at The Davids, which was built to house, and display the trophies. Many of the specimens were mounted by Rowland Ward and are recorded in the firm's published records of big game. During his visit to Alaska in 1911–12 Mr Laurence Cadbury had to shoot animals for food in order to survive. This started his interest in shooting, which in those days was regarded as legitimate sport. In 1934 he and his wife embarked on a three-month tour of Africa and kept a detailed record of their experiences. From Freetown in Sierra Leone they travelled down the West Coast to Lobito in Angola, crossed country to Rhodesia (Zimbabwe) before journeying north to Nairobi and the Victoria Falls. They returned to Croydon via Cairo, Milan and Paris. As the couple crossed the Equator, they noted that it is 'Not what one might expect. The temperature fell, we had our first rainstorm since leaving Liverpool and a gale of wind'. They returned with the above trophies, all except the moose, which came from Alaska. (*Sir Adrian Cadbury*)

The tankards in the dining-room are replicas of solid silver originals made in the seventeenth century, which were given by the Cadbury family to the Birmingham Museum and Art Gallery. On Thursday and Friday, 17 and 18 November 1988, a sale by auction took place, in a marquee on the premises, of the remaining contents of The Davids which had been the home of Mr and Mrs Laurence Cadbury's family for many years. (*Sir Adrian Cadbury*)

The Old Bell (or Bluebell) Inn, built in 1711, stood at the Junction of Bell Lane with Bell Holloway and, in the days of the stage-coach, served as a coaching station midway between the Hen & Chickens in Birmingham, and the Rose and Crown at the Lickeys. Here horses could be rested or the coachman take fresh horses for the remainder of his journey. A second coach route passed through Northfield and crossed the Birmingham–Bromsgrove road at the Inn. This road went from Stourbridge and the Black Country to Evesham and Stratford. Coaches followed

approximately the direction of Church Road as we know it today, round by Northfield Church and out to Alcester. In 1851 the occupants of the Old Bell Inn were Joseph and Edward Grove who were not only innkeepers, but also maltsters, master builders, brick makers and farmers employing 17 men. Presumably when the line of the road was altered, and trade was transferred to the new Inn, The Old Bell Inn became private property, as in the apportionment of rent charges for Northfield in 1839 it is described as 'House, Garden and Malthouse', and was then known as the Old Bell House. The house was demolished in the early 1960s. (*Cadbury Trebor Bassett*)

By the middle of the twentieth century much of the architecture of the Old Bell Inn was Georgian and the owners, Mr and Mrs J.F. Merry, furnished the rooms beautifully (as seen in these photographs). The eighteenth century recessed cupboard in the morning-room was built out from the wall and may possibly have been used for housing wine bottles brought up from the cellar. Note the Queen Anne love seat and the Chamberlain-Worcester china. (*Cadbury Trebor Bassett*)

The Inn dated from the time of Queen Anne and boasted a beautiful Queen Anne staircase. The treads were both wide and deep giving an impression of strength and dignity. The oak banister ran along the first-floor landing and the woodwork was continued in the arch, beyond which a vaulted ceiling can just be seen. (*Cadbury Trebor Bassett*)

The corner recess in this picture has been created where an old bookcase used to be and the fireplace is a replica of the original, installed when the Inn was built. Note the height of the windows and the old beam, which just appears in the picture. (*Cadbury Trebor Bassett*)

Hole Farm is a three-storied residential property in Hole Lane built of brick with a clay-tiled roof. It was once the property of the Garland Family who moved there from Handsworth in the early twentieth century and furnished it beautifully in the Victorian tradition. It still retains an outbuilding that would once have been used as stables and it is believed that the property was once a farmhouse, erected around the mid-eighteenth century. (*Birmingham Central Library*)

Hole Farm, boarded up and in a very dilapidated state, was sold by auction in the summer of 2001. (*J. Smith*)

John Gilbert and Edith Mary Garland celebrating their Golden Wedding in the grounds of Hole Farm in 1929. Back row, left to right: Ivor Hamel-Cooke, J. Ash Garland, Patrick J. Garland, Ian Hamel-Cooke. Second row: Elsie Garland, Dorothy G. Garland, John Gilbert Garland, Edith Mary Garland, Alwyn Hamel-Cooke, Marjorie K. Cooke. Front row: Christopher Hamel-Cooke, Priscilla Hamel-Cooke and Michael Garland. Miss Dorothy G. Garland, who lived at Hole Farm all her life, did not marry and the house eventually became hers. (*N. Hamel-Cooke*)

The drawing-room in Hole Farm with Bechstein piano and corner cabinet, which contained china. (*N. Hamel-Cooke*)

Miss Garland's bedroom on the top floor of Hole Farm. (*N. Hamel-Cooke*)

Miss Garland's sitting-room on the first floor over the dining-room. (*N. Hamel-Cooke*)

Digbeth Mill gave its name to, and stood in, Mill Lane, Northfield, and before the advent of engine-driven machinery, obtained its power from the River Rea flowing alongside. John and Anne Tomkins Morris, with their ten children, the youngest only a few months old, arrived at Digbeth Mill in 1880, having travelled from Ipsley Mill, Studley, on a farm cart with a cow in tow. The mill produced bran etc. for animal fodder, and when John died in 1883 his son Walter took over its running, converting part of the miller's house into a grocery shop. One of the last men to work it was Mr Walter C. Morris, of Steel Road, who, with his brother, Jack, took over the Mill after their father's death in 1921. The mill now produced flour and Walter used to supply special flour to the vicar of Northfield Parish. They found

that water power was unreliable, because of the difficulty of keeping up the level of the pool, and installed a steam engine, which was used to drive the grinding machinery when the water wheel was unable to do so. The engine was housed in the old stable, seen on the right of the shop in the drawing. When trade was slack the miller helped Albert Morton with funerals. Etching by J.H. Hipsley. (*C. Read*)

Jack Morris of Digbeth Mill at his wedding to Ruby Ward. The best man is Walter C. Morris. J.E. Morris and J. Ward owned the Central Corn and Seed Stores (Morris & Ward) selling dog foods and birdseed, as well as being high-class florists. They were described as 'Artists in Wreaths, Crosses and Floral Decorations' and supplied displays for all the local occasions such as baskets and posies for Tinkers Farm School's May Festival, displays for functions at the Woodlands Hospital and the Austin Conventions. Christine Read (née Morris) remembers seeing many floral tributes being prepared for Lord Austin's funeral. (*C. Read*)

The Great Stone Inn is one of the oldest licensed houses in the city and was originally built completely from stone. It was rebuilt with brick in the seventeenth century. The name is derived from the large boulder, which can be seen here on the north-east corner of the inn in a very narrow pavement, and was originally deposited by the movement of a glacier from the Arenig Mountains (several miles west of Lake Bala), North Wales, during the Ice Age. The present inn dates from around 1500, although there was an inn on the same site before that date. The innkeeper used not only to be the publican but also the butcher and victualler. In the seventeenth century it was listed as the venue for the Coroner's Court, and during the time of Cromwell, as a centre where certain administrative matters received attention. (*P. Tidey-Hamilton*)

As traffic increased the stone was felt to be a danger to traffic and pedestrians. Following residents' complaints that children and mothers with prams had to get off the pavement on to a narrow roadway at the blind ninety degree corner to go round the stone it was decided to remove it to the Pound, adjacent to the Great Stone Inn. Legend said it was over 14-ft deep, was part of the foundations of the Inn and had both historical and mystical qualities. This caused some dispute owing to the beliefs surrounding the stone, but eventually a crane capable of lifting 20 tons was brought in, the traffic was stopped for a day and preparations made to lift it. PC Robert C. Saunders was posted to control what little traffic there was while the work was carried out. (*J. Andrews*)

However, the Great Stone turned out to be only eight inches deep – little more than a pebble! (*J. Andrews*)

The stone in its new resting place in the Pound. There has been a Pound in Northfield since at least the fifteenth century, possibly earlier, and its position in Northfield points to the fact that this was once an agricultural area surrounded by farms and smallholdings. Built of sandstone, it was used for impounding stray cattle and horses from a radius of thirty miles, until the owners paid a modest fine to the local magistrate (usually the rector) for their return when appearing, together with witnesses, to prove their case at the next court. Occasionally local inhabitants did not wait for the next court to retrieve their animals and broke into the Pound. In 1439 the local Rector was caught committing this offence and not only retrieved his own beasts but took other people's too! The eighteenth century saw the introduction of poor boxes into the church in 1707. Previously there had been collections for the poor and needy. The unemployed, to obtain assistance, were obliged to stand for a specified time each day in the village pound. The Pound was a regular feature in many villages but Northfield is unique in that it is the only surviving manorial pound in Birmingham, and would originally have been one of at least twenty serving villages within the boundary of the present city. It is regarded as one of the finest pounds in England. (*O. Williams*)

Basically a medieval building, the old rectory was reconstructed by the Hinckley family during the reign of Queen Anne, *c.* 1705. It was again reconstructed in 1930, following examination of the survey in 1928 by the Dilapidations Committee as a result of the Dilapidation Act of 1923, which stated that all parsonages, etc. must be in a thorough state of repair. In the eighteenth century the rector's duties were not confined to church business only; the rector was also the Justice of the Peace. The court was held in a special room called the Court Room and plans of the rectory also show a school room. (*M. Banton*)

By the 1970s the old rectory was too expensive to run and far too large for the resident rector so it was decided to convert the building into a pastoral centre for the use of parishioners and the local community. A new, smaller rectory was built in the grounds next door to the old. (*J. Smith*)

The Pastoral Centre – 2001. Following the demolition of the wooden hut, which had been the original church hall, for a while the junior school hall was used as a parish hall, but this was not found to be satisfactory. Plans were drawn up for a parish centre on the site of church house in Church Hill, but planning permission was refused following objections from local residents and the problem of access and car parking. A scheme was then devised which involved the sale of the church house site to a housing association and the building of a new, smaller rectory. The church attempted to raise funds to create the Pastoral Centre from the old rectory, but the congregation were unable to reach the target. A wider fundraising net was spread for a scheme to enable the Pastoral Centre to become available to the whole of Northfield. A hall and toilets were built on the side of the old rectory but little other change was necessary. The Pastoral Centre houses the parish office and a licensed bar and is used for a wide variety of activities, groups and parish organisations. (*J. Smith*)

Bournville Light Operatic Society and members of the Birmingham Schools' Symphony Orchestra giving a fundraising concert at the Pastoral Centre in 1979. Proceeds went towards the cost of the orchestra's forthcoming visit to Frankfurt, one of Birmingham's twin cities. The authors can be seen on the extreme left, and second in from the left on the front row of vocalists. (*Bromsgrove Messenger*)

The front elevation plan of the house in Heath Road South being built for Mr and Mrs A. Street. The building was begun in March 1939 and completed, ready for them to occupy on their return from honeymoon in June of the same year. At that time this was the last house on the south side of the road and for the next fourteen years the land beyond was approached over a stile into a field which was low-lying land with a stream running through and cows grazing on it. (*A. Street*)

Foundations laid and walls beginning to show. Part of Victoria Common is to the left of the houses opposite. (*A. Street*)

The local policeman kept his eye on things during construction. (*A. Street*)

House virtually completed and visitors coming to view. (*A. Street*)

Tithe Barns were instituted in the Middle Ages, and were extremely rare in the Midlands. Before the dissolution of the monasteries during the reign of Henry VIII, the monastery, or abbey, took a proportion of each farmer's crops to augment church funds. A tenth part was taken, hence the word tithe, so that every tenth sheaf of corn went to the church. To store the tithes between seasons, barns were built, not necessarily beside the abbeys but in a convenient place, centrally situated for the farmers and manor

house of the district. The medieval tithe barns were frequently buildings of great beauty. Most of them are early fourteenth century and many of them suffered ill treatment in that troublesome period. The monks of Halesowen Abbey, who had close connections with the Grange and parish church, probably built the one at Northfield. It was tastefully converted into a dwelling house in the late 1950s by a Mr Charles Evans, director of a Birmingham printing block company, who remodelled the sixteenth century barn and made it his home. Before conversion took place it had been used as a headquarters for boy scouts, and during the Second World War by the Home Guard. The farm to which the barn originally belonged was known as Moat Farm, last occupied in 1801, and took its name from the moat with which it was surrounded. Today it gives its name to Old Moat Drive. (P. Tidey-Hamilton)

A conservation order came too late to save the tithe barn so in 1969 it was demolished and the James Park estate, comprising twenty-two semi-detached houses and twelve flats, was built on the site.
(O. Williams)

Middleton Hall. In the thirteenth century Middleton was one of the tithings of the manor of Northfield and Weoley, having been carved out of the chief manor in the latter half of the twelfth century. A John Mershton is recorded as having paid homage to the Lord of Weoley for his farm, which stood on the site of the later Middleton Hall. The hall was largely rebuilt in the early nineteenth century, and had a substantial part of the medieval building incorporated into its rear. Prior to 1840 Middleton Hall Farm was the largest in the district, and together with its Elizabethan barns proved an imposing site. It was situated at the corner of Bunbury Road with Woodlands Park Road, and, after becoming derelict, was demolished in 1955. (*Birmingham Central Library*)

In 1959 twenty freehold houses with garages were built on the site of Middleton Hall, and together with the eighteenth century coachman's cottage dated 1796 the twenty-one houses were called Redmead Close. During the building of these houses the foundations of a moat were discovered. (*J. Smith*)

In 1851 Street Farm is listed as being in the yield of Hay-with-Middleton and having 140 acres. It belonged to a William Newey who employed four labourers. In the nineteenth century each parish was sub-divided into yields making it easier to assess the output of cultivation for the purpose of taxation. In 1881 the farm still consisted of 140 acres and a Thomas Drakeley lived there with his wife and family. He too employed four men. Farmers living at Street Farm on Bunbury Road since then have included Miss Wilson, 'Billy' Field and Mr Blunn. Mrs Wyeth recalls fetching fresh eggs from the farm when she was a child and being taken round the back to see the hens. The photograph was taken c. 1957 and the farm was demolished in 1958. (M. Banton)

The Northfield YMCA now stands on land once occupied by Street Farm. It was opened on 11 October 1961 and in September 1965 further property was purchased. The YMCA is a national and international organisation, which has progressed rapidly since George Williams, in 1844, realised his vision of creating opportunities for young people to meet together. In Birmingham it provides a range of accommodation,

community, leisure and recreational facilities across the city and works closely with the Local Authority and other statutory and voluntary bodies to meet the needs of the community. During the last twelve months the Northfield YMCA has replaced the sports hall roof and refurbished the multi-gym. It houses squash courts, a sports hall, a community day care nursery, and coaches regular football groups for local youths. (J. Smith)

Councillor E.R. Canning JP laid the foundation stone of St Bartholomew's Church on 21 April 1937, and the opening and consecration of the new church took place on 7 May 1938. The church is on the Allen's Cross estate on the corner of Hoggs Lane and Allens Farm Road, but is temporarily out of use as it suffered a serious fire in 1998. Services at present are being held in the chapel at the Hollymoor Centre, pending a decision on the building of a new church. The Allen's Cross estate was built in 1927–8 in order to help absorb some of the excess population moving out of the city centre. The estate is named after the farm, which was on the site now occupied by St Bartholomew's Church. (*J. Baker*)

About 1980, to celebrate St Bartholomew's day in August, the vicar and choir of St Bartholomew's Church, in vestments and gowns, processed around parts of the parish carrying the cross. (*J. Baker*)

Steel Road altar hut, *c.* 1920. Following the use of a recreation hut inside the gate of the west works at the Austin Motor Company and the occasional use of a clubroom at the rear of the Black Horse for early morning mass, in 1918 Mr P. Shea of Small Heath gave £150 towards the building of a new church asking the archbishop to name it St Bridget's as he

was an Irishman. In March 1918 the Archdiocese bought a house in Steel Road and named it St Bride's. The house and altar were furnished, the two main rooms being converted into a through-room where services were held. In December 1918 a wooden hut with a corrugated iron roof was obtained and erected in the back garden of Steel Road to be used as a chapel. This was uncomfortably hot in summer and draughty in winter. (*T. Battle*)

Second church of Our Lady and St Brigid. By 1930 a new building was needed and two acres of land were bought in Cock Lane, (Frankley Beeches Road after 1932) at a cost of £1,500. As was usual at that time a hall was built which could serve both as church and parish hall. The men of the parish helped with the building work and it was completed in March 1931, cost £2,500 and was dedicated to Our Lady and St Brigid. The hut was brought from Steel Road and re-erected behind the brick hall/church where it was also known as the 'clubroom' or even the 'pavilion'. (*T. Hill*)

Third church of Our Lady and St Brigid. Because of the increase in local housing estates, factory and hospital populations increased rapidly and a larger church was soon needed. The foundation stone of the present church was laid on 1 February 1936 and the opening took place on 30 November that year, thus the first, second and third parish churches dedicated to Our Lady and St Bride (Brigid) were now brought together on one site. It appears from an access viewpoint to be facing the 'wrong way', but it was built this way so that its architectural beauty would be seen and easy access gained to the church hall and the proposed new school. The second church is now the school hall. (*T. Battle*)

Resurrection in the church of Our Lady and St Brigid. The mural was commissioned by Our Lady and St Brigid to fill the apse, a 25-ft high domed recess behind the altar, lighting the 100-ft nave, and has taken Neil Harvey nine years to paint, somewhat longer than originally anticipated. Problems have been encountered such as the curvature of the wall's surface making the perspective difficult to accomplish. This necessitated making extensive life drawings and a big scale plaster model of his ideas prior to beginning. His working hours were also restricted by the need to work in natural light. Neil wanted to do something that reacted against the reductionism of modern church art, and hopes that it will last as long as Renaissance work. His work depicts Christ rising heavenwards before four Roman guards who watch in awe and astonishment. Prior to beginning the wall was in such a state with peeling paint and large damp patches it took Neil two years to prepare its surface. To perfect his plaster base he was sent by English Heritage to Rome where he learned from the Vatican of a formula of lime putty made from crushed Carrara marble laced with linseed oil, a recipe unused for 400 years, which came from a sixteenth-century painter, Girolamo Muziano. Neil says the finished painting borrows something from the Renaissance, with his own neo-Baroque modernity. He hopes it will bring 'a sense of hope and joy to those who visit'. (© *The Artist, N. Harvey*)

Set well back in Meeting House Lane, off Church Road, The Friends' Meeting House was first used on 25 February 1930. The building, completed at a total cost (including the garden layout, the approach road, drainage, and so on) of £3,400, was built on a plot of ground given to the meeting by George Cadbury, Senior. Since 1930 a classroom and a kitchen have been added. The original 'official' home of Northfield Friends was The Institute, first used for meetings for worship in June 1892. Meetings were held in the large upstairs room facing Church Road and along the whole of this left-hand frontage, above the ground floor windows, were engraved the words 'FRIENDS MEETING HOUSE'. Until recently the present meeting house also performed a most useful social service in that it was used by a number of organisations for their weekly events. Two adult schools are associated with the meeting; a men's school – which was founded by George Cadbury, Senior, about 1895, and a women's school, formed by Dame Elizabeth Cadbury – on the grounds that if the men could have a school the women could also! (*E. Pickvance*)

Northfield Friends' Silver Jubilee Meeting – 1955. The building itself may be unobtrusive – even unnoticed, but, like the church, its strength and power spring from its membership. Within its walls have worshipped a number of men and women who have given life-long service to the community; as councillors, magistrates, hospital and school governors, social and industrial workers, doctors and teachers. (*E. Pickvance*)

Northfield Baptist Church. Due to the expansion of Northfield around 1911, brought about by the building of the railway station, a few local Baptists held services in the village hall in Woodlands Park Road, where afternoon Sunday school soon followed, and subsequently a church, with twenty-two members, was formed on 4 June 1912. In November 1915, due to the generosity of George Cadbury, who leased land rent free, a new black and white church building was erected in Bunbury Road (opposite Rathvilly School) at a cost of £421. The erection of a large number of wooden bungalows by Austin during the First World War prompted the members to share in opening a branch church there in 1921. In 1931 the church at Longbridge became a separate fellowship. By 1933 trams running through Northfield helped the development of the Allens Cross estate and a Sunday School began there using private houses, the community centre and Tinkers Farm schools. In 1935 the Revd Henry Royston was offered the pastorate but before accepting insisted the church move to a more central site. The new Bristol Road church and schoolrooms were opened in 1937, and the church at last had a baptistry. The original church building was moved to Bristol Road and served as a YWCA canteen during the Second World War, then as a Sunday School, and later as a youth centre before being destroyed by fire in 1971. (*J. Upton*)

Northfield Baptist Church and Ash Grove. Following the Second World War the church played an important part in the birth of the ecumenical movement in Northfield and the establishment of the Northfield Council of Churches. In 1964 the Sunday School was closed and the children's work incorporated into the morning family worship. This, together with a growth of needs in other areas of the church's work, emphasised the need for a new building, and on Saturday, 5 February 1972, in the Church's Diamond Jubilee year, the opening ceremony and dedication of the new church was performed by Mr Michael Cadbury, having been built at a cost of £34,000. Over 400 people attended the ceremony. Following completion of the new premises, the idea was suggested of building sheltered accommodation (in conjunction with the Baptist Housing Society) adjacent to the church and, in November 1986, Ash Grove, reflecting the name of Ash Bank Farm, (which originally owned the site of the church) was opened. The scheme provided warden controlled flats for forty-five people, and completed the development of the site for the Church's 75th Jubilee Anniversary. (*J. Smith*)

The first Northfield Methodist Church photographed in 1926. Records indicate the presence of a Wesleyan Methodist Chapel in Northfield from 1841, but the actual whereabouts of such a building is open to debate. The Bristol Road South/Chatham Road site for the above church was purchased and a school chapel erected in the spring of 1899. Indication of the growth of the society is given when in 1906 the men's Sunday afternoon Bible class, together with other organisations in the church, felt the need for enlarged facilities, so a new room was built and other renovations carried out. The chapel was licensed for the solemnization of marriages in 1914. In 1925 a plot of land next to the chapel was bought with the intention of building a new church, schools and tennis courts. The original church is fondly remembered for its warmth of friendship and depth of spiritual life. (*A. Green*)

The second Northfield Methodist Church photographed in 1956. The Wesleyan Methodist Church on the corner of Bristol Road and Benacre Street was bombed in the Second World War. Because of this, and the feeling at Northfield that their existing church was now inadequate for the needs of the expanding suburb, it was decided not to rebuild on the Benacre Street site, but to replace the damaged church with a new building adjacent to the existing Northfield Methodist Church. The rescued door arch of the Benacre Street Church was to be incorporated as the entrance to a Memorial Chapel. In 1953 an application was submitted and war damage compensation of £57,000 (enhanced by an appeal for £12,000 to build an impressive church and suite of premises) was granted for the building of the new church at Northfield. The old church remained in use until the new church was completed. (*R. de Boer*)

The third Northfield Methodist Church. In the 1980s it became apparent that the size and financial demands of the premises were draining the resources and curtailing the real work of the church. After much debate, prayer and heart-searching it was decided to sell the front part of the site, including the church itself, to a developer and re-model the remaining premises to provide a more manageable worship centre which could better serve the needs of both the congregation and the local community. In October 1987 the congregation vacated the church, but continued to worship in the concert hall until June 1988 when redevelopment commenced. Services in the intervening period were held at St Laurence Pastoral Centre and Hay Green Methodist Church. Most church activities and meetings continued with each group making its own arrangements for suitable venues and much co-operation, hospitality and kindness was received from other churches in the circuit and the area. (*Dr E.D. Graham*)

The front of the site is now occupied by Charlie Brown's Autocentres for spare parts. (*J. Smith*)

An aerial shot of Hollymoor Hospital when it was a working mental hospital. Originally opened as an annexe to Rubery Mental Hospital in 1905, Hollymoor was the third lunatic asylum to be built in Birmingham. The first was at Winson Green (later known as All Saints) and the second, in 1882, at Rubery Hill. By 1905 it was felt that the best treatment for the mentally ill was clean country air so patients were first admitted to Winson Green then, following assessment and treatment, transferred to Rubery Hill or Hollymoor. In 1915 both Rubery Hill and Hollymoor were converted to hospitals for wounded soldiers, being known as the First Birmingham War Hospital, Rednal and the Second Birmingham War Hospital, Northfield respectively. In January 1918 it was again converted into a special military hospital for Orthopaedic cases with most of the necessary splints and bed frames being made in workshops set up on the premises. The last soldiers left in 1921 when the building was restored to its original purpose and re-opened as an asylum in 1922. From 1942 to 1948, Hollymoor was used as a military psychiatric hospital treating wounded soldiers from Dunkirk, Australia, Canada, New Zealand, West Africa, Belgium, Holland and Poland, as well as prisoners of war. During this time group therapy was introduced which proved very successful. Also admitted were sick and injured civilians from south coast towns, and people from Birmingham injured in the blitz. Hollymoor Mental Hospital, Northfield was re-opened as a separate hospital on 24 June 1950. (*West Northfield Comm. Ass. Ltd, Hollymoor Centre*)

Hollymoor Hospital after demolition, *c.* 1994. In 1988 the *Birmingham Post* reported that four Birmingham hospitals were to close and most of the 250-acre site on which they stood was to be sold for redevelopment. Some 800 houses, a shopping complex, a health centre, community facilities and a business centre were to replace the Rubery Hill, Hollymoor, John Conolly and Joseph Sheldon Hospitals. The redevelopment of the land was to enable a comprehensive modernisation of health services in the Midlands to take place, this redevelopment being in stages and the money raised used for the care of mentally ill patients in Birmingham and Solihull and to improve the distribution of beds for the elderly. The last patients left Hollymoor in July 1994, with most of the hospital being demolished in 1995–6. (*West Northfield Comm. Ass. Ltd, Hollymoor Centre*)

The green dome of the water tower at Hollymoor Hospital became a familiar local landmark. The tower pumped water from the Frankley reservoirs to provide general water supplies as well as heating for the hospital via hot pipes and steam radiators. The hospital was totally self-contained, with all patients who were able to, working to maintain the various departments. It had its own chapel for religious services, library run by Red Cross and St John organisations, cinema, dances, handicrafts, Darby & Joan Club, art, English and PT classes, shops and hairdressers. It ran its own farm for dairy products, kitchens, bakery (which also supplied Rubery Hill), laundry, greenhouses, potting sheds, and gardens, and it kept pigs. (*West Northfield Comm. Ass. Ltd, Hollymoor Centre*)

Sovereign Heights – part of the housing estate built on the site of Hollymoor Hospital. The water tower, which at present is derelict, is a listed building and there is a possibility it may become a health centre for the local community. (*J. Smith*)

In the main hall of Hollymoor Hospital all types of activities took place – table tennis, badminton, film shows, social evenings, dances, whist drives, plays, variety shows and concerts given by orchestras, brass bands, choral societies and amateur operatic groups. The authors both remember visiting there in the early 1960s, as members of the Bournville Amateur Operatic Society, to entertain the patients. In 1965 a day hospital was opened where patients attended for treatment during the day but returned home at night. This enhanced the treatment patients were able to receive as out-patients, and often enabled in-patients to return home earlier than they would otherwise have been able to do. In 1969 a special unit for mentally ill adolescents was opened, providing beds for ten male and ten female patients. (*West Northfield Comm. Ass. Ltd, Hollymoor Centre*)

During its time as a mental hospital the chapel, in addition to holding religious services, played an important part in the life of Hollymoor Hospital as a place of refuge and comfort to the disturbed. Today it remains important to the local community. The Hollymoor Centre is a group of modern offices, training areas and meeting spaces within the Victorian elegance of the reception and chapel building of the former hospital. The buildings have been extensively refurbished and equipped to create a Media Training Centre and performance hall. The centre provides training in state-of-the-art, high-tech multi-media skills, including not only TV and video, radio, recording, journalism and graphics, but also in the new multi-media world of telematics and super-highways. It also houses a community nursery, catering and an employment resource centre. The Old Chapel's superb acoustics have been augmented by the latest digital sound equipment and a full lighting rig to television production standard, giving an extremely flexible and spacious, yet intimate atmosphere.
(*J. Smith*)

In 1881 the Priory was owned by an Anglican family called Stock who were dealers in steel and stained glass. A benevolent family, Thomas Stock had five daughters who were *the* ladies of the village. They would sit up all night with any child who was ill to save the mother losing her sleep and would provide baby clothes when parents were too poor to provide them themselves. Mr Stock gave the house to the diocese who sold it to a Mr Poncia

for £3,000 who then returned it to the diocese to be used as a charitable institution. The diocese then asked the Order of our Lady of Charity in Bartestree, Hereford to start a foundation there in 1905. Five sisters came from Bartestree and founded the House of Our Lady of Charity, where, from the Priory, they cared for the sick and disadvantaged. The main building was gradually added to and when full to capacity (as it often was) it accommodated ninety women and girls. Girls and women who needed care and protection were brought to the convent and it was decided to teach them needlework. This was not successful so a laundry was begun to provide therapeutic work for the girls and women, which catered for all the laundry needs of the Woodlands Hospital and some in the local community, and was also a necessary source of income. (*T. Battle*)

The Priory – 2001. Towards the end of the twentieth century the Priory became too expensive to maintain, and it was not a viable proposition to convert it for modern use, so, around 1980, a new Priory was built and with great sadness the old one vacated and demolished. Fond memories still exist of the old building, such as Dame Elizabeth Cadbury visiting each Christmas and providing the Sisters with jam and chocolates. Approximately twelve Sisters live there today. (*J. Smith*)

In the 1960s Kalamazoo was recognised as one of the leading British firms producing recording and accounting equipment and supplying all kinds of stationery and equipment used for clerical work in general, but particularly for book-keeping and recording purposes. In 1890 Oliver Morland acquired small premises in Edmund Street, Birmingham where he set up a general printing business specializing in coloured wrappers and labels. In 1900 his cousin, Paul Impey, joined him

and together they looked for ways of expanding the business. In 1904, while visiting America, Mr Morland saw a new style of loose leaf binder which was far less clumsy and heavy than ones used in England, so the partners took up the selling agency for the binder made by the Loose Leaf Binder Company in Kalamazoo, a town in the state of Michigan, USA. As business flourished more space became necessary and in 1907 larger premises were taken in Barwick Street. However, dissatisfaction with the quality of the American binders prompted the partners to manufacture their own product and so the company of Morland and Impey Ltd was formed in 1908. Trade slowly but steadily expanded at home and abroad and by 1912 the Barwick Street premises became too small, so the site of the present factory in Northfield was purchased and the company moved into their new premises in 1913. (*Birmingham Central Library*)

Part of the factory in Mill Lane is now closed down and boarded up. In 1919–20 the original factory was greatly extended and as time went by the scope of products increased. From 1920 the firm traded under two names – Morland and Impey Ltd selling binders with printed sheets being sold through Kalamazoo (Sales) Ltd. In 1943 it was decided to merge the two companies into Kalamazoo Ltd. By 1945 when Oliver Morland retired, the company had grown to be one of the leading printing concerns in the country. In the postwar years, to meet the demands of a rapidly expanding business, a large modern factory was completed in 1962. In 1967 Kalamazoo set up its own Computer Services Division and operates one of Europe's largest computer bureaux, sells sophisticated systems, and has been training its own and its clients' staff ever since. (*J. Smith*)

A photograph of the Hole Farm development taken in 1970. The Hole Farm estate development started in 1966. Detached, semi-detached and terraced houses were built. Bungalows and houses were constructed on Heath Road South and Hole Farm Road, and two- and three-storey flats for the Cornfield Housing Society were also erected. Flats were built with money borrowed from the Housing Corporation. The Cornfield Housing Society was a co-ownership society sponsored by BVT. Trustees handed over the running of the society to a Committee of Management in 1970 on completion of the scheme. (*O. Williams*)

The same scene as it looks in 2001. Many local people had been very sad to see this area developed for, as Mrs E. Pickvance recalls, 'It was a really wild area of natural beauty with an unmade pond, beautiful May hedges and an abundance of lovely wild flowers. A botanist's delight and a wonderful natural play area for local children with plenty of bushes to hide in.' In 1988 a five-year plan began which included a major refurbishment of the Garland Way Pool and surrounding area. (*J. Smith*)

2

Around the Village

The smithy stood at the corner of Bristol Road South and Church Road until a few years before the war. The blacksmith at one time was one Isaac Tongue. This character was known for his 'christening' ceremonies over the anvil. Youngsters were taken to his forge after their official baptism and given a nickname by which they were known locally for the rest of their lives. Very few true Northfield people were known by other than the sobriquet given them by Mr Tongue, and a clergyman new to the district once called upon a life long resident to ask for the *real* names of his flock. Later John Cole & Son owned the cottage and forge. (*Birmingham Central Library*)

Huins Corner at the junction of Bristol Road South and Bell Hill was so-called because of Huins shoe shop, which stood there. Pam Hambidge recalls 'It was one of the first shops in Birmingham to install an X-ray machine, which showed the bones of the feet and the sole of the shoes to see they fitted correctly. On the opposite side of the road, next door to Woolworths, was a shoe repair shop in which a lady sat in the window repairing ladders in ladies' nylon stockings.' Arthur Hodge recalls how he and his sister used to recite a poem about the shops in Northfield: – 'J.J. Davis, Tailor Moores, Huins Shoes and Humble's Stores.' (*T. Hill*)

The same corner as it looks today, Huins and all the other shops mentioned now long gone. (*S. Barnes*)

Parsons Woodyard stood on the corner of Church Road and Bristol Road South, its distinguishing feature being a wooden windmill standing on its forecourt. Mr W.B. Parsons founded the timber and carpentry business, which was later managed by his sons. He was organist and choirmaster of the little wooden Methodist church, which stood for many years opposite the Black Horse. Together with his wife he later joined the Society of Friends and became the superintendent of the Sunday School and choirmaster of the institute choir. (*T. Hill*)

The Grosvenor Shopping Centre under construction. Development of the proposed site began in 1966 when the major part of the basement was constructed. However, the original developers withdrew and cancelled their commission to the architects. When the Grosvenor Estate Development took over it was aware of the need for a major shopping centre in Northfield to serve one of the most under-shopped districts in the Birmingham region with a catchment area then of more than 130,000 people. The original architects, Halpern and Partners, were

commissioned to produce a new design that would use the almost completed existing basement structure. A large vehicle service and delivery area takes up most of the space below ground. With most of the shops facing inwards, to combat a monotonous blank appearance along the long street frontage, the exterior was clad in metallic green moulded fibreglass panels, striking in appearance and trouble free in maintenance. P&O Shopping Centres bought the centre in June 1988 and acquired the car park above from Birmingham City Council in August 1992. The car park holds 700 vehicles and is an asset to the centre with low parking costs. (*O. Williams*)

The second Bell Inn. Prior to 1790 the Bristol Road ran past the Old Bell Inn and along Bell Lane. In 1790 an act empowered the trustees to make a new and improved line for the Bristol Road from Woodbrooke to the Pigeon House, causing the Old Bell Inn to be by-passed. Shortly after this, in 1803–4, a public house known as the Bell Inn was erected on the site of the present Bell Inn. Before the act this site was part of the Bromsgrove Turnpike Road. The Bell Inn in the photograph was rebuilt between 1897 and 1901 and was a familiar landmark on Bristol Road South. It comprised four bars and a clubroom, and was owned by Davenports. (*D. Mayo*)

The third Bell Inn – closed and in a state of dereliction. In 1982–3 the brewers decided the second inn was too large and uneconomical to run and should be replaced with a smaller pub, so the site of the old pub was sold for the development of shops and the inn demolished. The new pub, to be built next door and called the Bell Inn, was to have a lounge and public bar, with a surprise feature on the outside, which turned out to be a large brass bell! (*J. Smith*)

Ash Bank Farm with lovely pink hawthorn trees in front. Many people remember the pretty garden, and the family delivering milk in a pony and trap ladling the milk out of a churn. Pat Tidey-Hamilton recalls, as a youngster, collecting milk from Ash Bank Farm when it was sold straight from the cow. In the early 1950s the fair came annually to the farm, an event much looked forward to by the youth of the area. In 1952 Birmingham City Council acquired the farmhouse and land by a compulsory purchase order for the purpose of building the relief road to by-pass the village centre. Joyce Brown and her mother left the property in 1958 and the farmhouse was demolished. (*P. Tidey-Hamilton*)

Since the demolition of Ash Bank Farm the shops adjacent to the MEB (now Powerhouse) have occupied the site on which it stood. (*J. Smith*)

Bristol Road South, *c.* 1958. Many people have fond recollections of Smallwoods, the wonderful hardware shop on the left of the picture, with its smell of polish, paraffin and linseed oil; also Wheeler's garage whose owner Mr Tom Wheeler was a character worthy of mention. Most of his life had been spent building horse-drawn vehicles, but with the coming of the car he founded a garage in the centre of the village. It seems it was then a common sight to see Mr Wheeler washing down the cars he eventually owned and whistling to them just as if they were horses. (Apparently, as they brush a horse's coat, ostlers whistle to prevent dust entering their mouths.) (*K. Wright*)

The scene today, where shops in the centre of the village suffer greatly from vandalism and many have unsightly steel shutters, covered in graffiti, to protect their doors and windows when closed. Local people have expressed concern that Northfield has become vulnerable to decline and is suffering from a lack of investment. A Northfield Local Action Plan, drawn up in consultation with the local community, was adopted in June 2000. It sets out the framework for the physical and economic regeneration of Northfield. In March 2001, details of a £16 million scheme for the regeneration of Northfield Centre were announced to the public, with funding coming partly from central Government, as part of the Local Transport Plan settlement, and partly from the sale of the Frankley Beeches Road Depot site. The plan is to stimulate development, revitalise the town centre and create an attractive and healthy environment. (*J. Smith*)

The south side of Bristol Road South in the centre of the village showing cottages converted to shops. The Roman road known as the Upper Saltway, which site the Bristol Road probably now occupies, was used mainly for conveying salt from Droitwich to the Lincolnshire Coast and from thence to Europe, for the use of Roman soldiers engaged in fighting. In the early 1900s cottages with gardens stood where the shops now stand on both sides of the road, and Pam Chiswell remembers when she was small seeing women sitting out on wooden kitchen chairs in short front gardens. Since 1908 the road has been widened considerably, and pavements added, by taking in the gardens of the cottages. In 1908 cyclists were prosecuted for riding 'furiously' if they exceeded 15 mph. (*O. Williams*)

The same view in the late 1990s when the cottages had been demolished and replaced by Argos, Specsavers and the Halifax Building Society. Due to increasing congestion through the centre of Northfield, the largest part of the current proposals for regeneration is the provision of a relief road, (a scheme which has been suggested for approximately fifty years). It is proposed that, together with construction of a relief road, the swimming baths will be refurbished, a new Sainsbury's superstore will be built on the site of the former Frankley Beeches Road depot, there will be environmental improvements to the town centre, (such as tree planting, improved street furniture and pavements, more pedestrian crossings and traffic calming,) and improvements to Victoria Common. (*J. Smith*)

Elm Cottage. In the days of Cromwell the Red Lion Inn was one of the earliest inns on the Bristol Road, possibly dating from the latter part of the seventeenth century. Mr Thomas Hunt who owned the land on which two other features of Northfield's history were built (the tollhouse and the cinema) bought the premises in about 1875, when they were being used as a general store, and converted them into a private house. The lettering 'Red Lion' was built into the outhouse when bricks were re-used during the alterations. The dwelling house became known as Elm Cottage, and was the home of Miss Fanny Darby, granddaughter of Mr Hunt, and her cousin Mrs A.C. Chapman. Elm Cottage was demolished in 1985 and replaced by shops. Ash Grove, warden controlled homes for the elderly, was erected at the rear in part of the former garden. (*O. Williams*)

The site of the former Red Lion inn /Elm Cottage which has been replaced by the Woolwich Building Society and The British Heart Foundation shop. Funspot has now replaced Austins. (*J. Smith*)

The Toll House. Built of stone in 1601, the Toll House was originally situated opposite the junction with West Park Avenue, but maps after 1830 show it to be opposite the junction with the present Lockwood Road. The actual toll payable at a turnpike gate varied according to the type of vehicle and the breadth of its wheels. A cart with wide wheels was thought to do less damage to the road surface than one with a

narrow gauge rim and was, therefore, charged less. Tolls also had to be paid on all animals being driven along the road. The income from a busy Turnpike Road was quite high and the Trustees could rely on receiving, every Lady Day, some interest on their investment. In 1847 the income from the Birmingham to Bromsgrove Turnpike amounted to £1,786 9s 8d which, after expenditure, gave a balance of £380. The Toll House was demolished in 1923 in order to widen the road for the tramcars to Rubery and Rednal. (T. Hill)

There have been frequent changes in the shops now standing on the site where the Toll House once stood, but, because of increasing vandalism, in June 2001 the Birmingham Evening Mail reported that Cadbury Trebor Bassett had agreed to support a project, which would see hi-tech CCTV cameras installed in Northfield shopping centre, to boost a crime-fighting surveillance scheme. The total amount of funding is expected to be in the region of several thousand pounds. £35,000 a year is needed to run this scheme for at least three years. The CCTV scheme is a vital part of the £16 million plans to regenerate Northfield. (J. Smith)

The NORTHFIELD CINEMA

BRISTOL ROAD SOUTH

'Phone : Priory 1463.   *Proprietors :* NORTHFIELD PICTURES, LTD.

Secretary and Manager : H. C. PICKERING

TIMES AND PRICES OF ADMISSION
(*Including Tax*)

MATINEES—MONDAYS, THURSDAYS and SATURDAYS at 2.30 p.m. Doors open at 2.15 p.m.
Reduced Prices : BALCONY 9d.; STALLS 6d. and 4d

EVENINGS—CONTINUOUS. Doors open 6.0 p.m.
BALCONY 1/- and 1/3 ; STALLS 6d. and 9d.
SATURDAYS CONTINUOUS from 6.0 p.m. Doors open 5.45 p.m. BALCONY 1/3 ; STALLS 6d. and 9d.

No Half-prices on Saturday, Sunday Evenings or Bank Holidays.

CAR PARKING SPACE UNLIMITED

NOTICE—

Whilst every precaution is taken to protect Patrons' property, the Management accept no liability whatsoever for any theft or damage to motor cars, motor cycles, or other vehicles, while parked on the Cinema Car Park. Persons using the Car Park as a right of way do so at their own risk.

LOST PROPERTY.
Any Article lost in the Cinema should be claimed within one month.

IF YOU ARE NOT ALREADY ON OUR MAILING LIST FOR THIS MONTHLY PROGRAMME PLEASE LEAVE YOUR NAME AND ADDRESS AT THE PAY BOX

SUBJECT TO SLIGHT ALTERATION OR TRANSPOSITION WHEN RENDERED NECESSARY BY UNFORESEEN CIRCUMSTANCES

Under the management of Harold Cecil Pickering, Northfield cinema opened on 4 February 1929 with *The Triumph of the Scarlet Pimpernel*, starring Matheson Lang. It had a seating capacity of 1,200, a first class orchestra under the direction of Arthur Montgomery, and a shelter along one side to protect the public from the elements while queuing to enter. Prices of admission ranged from 6d to 1s 6d. It closed on 2 June 1962 and was later demolished to make way for more shops. Following the war years a British restaurant was opened next door to the cinema where nutritious and cheap meals could be obtained. (*T. Hill*)

A poster showing times, prices of admission and general information for cinemagoers. (*Birmingham Central Library*)

Hodge's Garage. Walter & William Hodge, both Birmingham Councillors and JPs, and their brother Alfred started the garage known as C.J. & A.E. Hodge around the turn of the nineteenth century. It stood on the corner of Cock Lane (now Frankley Beeches Road) with Bristol Road South. Arthur (known as Art, seen here on the right) and his cousin Christopher took over the garage, c. 1930. Prior to his marriage in 1935 Art left to work as a public contractor for the council, and Christopher continued to run the garage. The photograph shows an electric petrol pump being fitted to replace the old wind-up pump. Christopher's motorcar is in the background. Note the cinema in the background on the right of the photograph, which had been financed by Walter, William and Alfred Hodge. They also owned the shops adjoining the garage along Frankley Beeches Road, which have now been demolished. (*A. Hodge*)

Hodge's old garage building still stands on the same spot and a car and van hire company operates in the yard. The little Portakabin on the extreme left of the photograph is a chemist's shop. (*J. Smith*)

These delightful old cottages on Bristol Road South, opposite the Traveller's Rest pub were built in the early nineteenth century and were occupied until 1968. By 1969 they were vacant awaiting demolition for the building of the Grosvenor Shopping Centre. In 1937 one of the cottages sold flowers, then further along towards the village were a few shops and a space where Mr Dews sold second-hand cars. He also ran a café used frequently by van and lorry drivers, and known as Smoky Joes. (*O. Williams*)

Today the Grosvenor Shopping Centre towers over the site with the exit to the car park above it at the near end of where the cottages stood. (*J. Smith*)

The Traveller's Rest pub at Northfield as it was originally built with a very unsuitable thatched roof. Not long after it was built a fire occurred in the thatch and the blackened beams still remain there to this day. In 1929 Mitchells & Butlers, the brewers at the time, produced a postcard of the pub as a promotional item in connection with their Jubilee celebrations. It has been recalled by several people that in the early days of the Austin Motor Co., road testers tested cars along the Bristol Road stopping first at the Black Horse and then at the Traveller's Rest pubs to 'refresh' themselves before embarking upon the return journey. (D. Mayo)

The Traveller's Rest pub remains but some of the cottages have now gone and others have been converted into shops. The thatch was replaced with tiles. Today the Traveller's Rest belongs to Bass Leisure Retail, but according to the plans for the new relief road is due to be demolished. (J. Smith)

These cottages, standing at the top of Church Road, opposite to Mass Road, were demolished in the late 1960s to make way for the building of Millfield below. (*M. Broomfield*)

Around 1970 warden controlled flats (to be known as Millfield) were under construction in Church Road. The joint responsibility of the Housing and Welfare Committees, they were built to provide homes for fifty-eight elderly people in one-person and two-person flats, under the supervision of a warden. There is a communal lounge, small kitchen and quiet rooms, and a guest room adjoining the warden's flat, where relatives can stay in the case of illness among the residents. (*J. Smith*)

The original Northfield Library was a small building in Church Road, which had cost £750 to build with the foundation stone being laid in 1906. On 12 February 1914 Mr E. Jinks, who lived in a cottage opposite, first noticed fire in the library, but by the time the Northfield Fire Brigade arrived the blaze was so fierce they had to send for reinforcements from Kings Heath. Soon after their arrival the roof and ventilating shaft, with its heavy metal top, fell in. It was assumed to be the work of suffragettes as a note was found on a spike of the railings at the rear saying 'Give Women the Vote', together with a brown paper parcel

containing a book by Miss Christabel Pankhurst on which was written, 'To start your new library'. The library was rebuilt by the Free Libraries Committee and opened in 1914, the joint architects being C. Bateman and Alfred Hall. Excluding the Central and Sutton Coldfield Libraries, Northfield is currently the busiest community library in the city. It has a book fund of approximately £30,000 per annum, carries a stock of approximately 35,000 books and issues nearly 227,000 a year. (*J. Smith*)

The Friends' Meeting House, opened in 1892, containing a coffee tavern, known as the Cyclist's Arms, an assembly hall, a schoolroom, a billiard room and a double skittle-alley, together with a small kitchen, and a caretaker's house. For a period of about thirty-five years the Society of Friends used the large upstairs room and the main hall for worship and business, and a Sunday School also met there. The building was developed as a community centre, catering for all ages and interests, with many organisations meeting under its roof. In the early 1900s education

was a luxury denied to many, hence the development of adult schools. This meant people came to the building, much as they do today, to improve their knowledge and to meet people. By 1919 it had become known as the Northfield Village Institute. The Birmingham Harmonic Male Choir, founded the same year, the Northfield Prize Silver Band and the Girl Guides met there. Whist drives, concerts, lectures and public and political meetings, including two packed meetings at which Christabel Pankhurst was the principal speaker, took place. It has always been requisitioned on polling days for municipal and general elections, and a room used to be rented twice a week for the use of the Relieving Officer. The Registrar for Births and Deaths rented a room once a week for several years, and it became a receiving and distributing centre for a laundry. Billiards were the main attraction for a Men's Social Club which met on most week-days, but attendance dropped dramatically during the 1914–18 war years, sadly some of its members never returning to play again. (*J. Smith*)

Northfield Village Institute and Post Office. The Coffee Tavern, which was the only tea room in the village for ten years, closed down through lack of customers, but re-opened during the First World War as a popular billiard room for the use of wounded soldiers from Hollymoor Hospital. In 1921 a boys club was begun by the caretaker, which opened five nights a week with one mixed evening. There were cricket teams, football teams and a brass band

thus youth work began to grow in The Institute with the caretaker playing a prominent role, and this continued until the building was handed over to the Education Authority in 1951. Around this time St Laurence School used three rooms as classrooms while they awaited the building of the new junior school. During the Second World War the premises became the District Rest Centre for the suburb of Northfield. It was used for air-raid emergencies with men, women and children, several dogs and a few caged birds being sheltered there, some from as far away as London. In addition people from Coventry, and from Hole Lane (when the dropping of an oil bomb necessitated the evacuation of their homes) slept there for several nights. (*T. Hill*)

Northfield Adult Education Centre and Oulsnams. The first caretakers at Northfield Village Institute were Mr and Mrs Hill who also 'kept the Post Office'. The post office, formerly part of a villa on the main road, had been transferred to the end room on the ground floor of The Institute. Later, the post office was again transferred to the adjacent new building now occupied by Oulsnams the estate agents, before moving to

its present location on Bristol Road South. By 1951 Northfield Village Institute had fallen into a state of disrepair and in June of that year it was presented as a gift to the Education Department of Birmingham Corporation for educational purposes. Its potential as an adult education centre was soon realised, and by the mid-1970s the classes had increased vastly. The name was changed to Northfield Adult Education Centre, and it continues most successfully under that guise to the present day. (*J. Smith*)

treet Cottages in Church Road, which were formerly lived in by Nailers. The first record of a trade in the parish is of the baptism of a Nailer's daughter in 1594. By 1727 there were 122 nail makers working in the parish and the trade flourished until the outbreak of war in 1914. Many workers were engaged in nail making on a seasonal basis when work in the fields was impossible due to bad weather. However, due to exploitation, even full time nailers were extremely poor. The nails were normally manufactured in small forges, either in, or attached to, the nail maker's cottage. The nailer would be expected to equip himself with the simple tools he required (an 'oliver' comprising two hammers and an anvil in which were fixed various dies for cutting different types of nail) and the fuel for the forge. Conditions in the forge were hot and unpleasant and work frequently continued far into the night with all the family joining in, the babies being placed in baskets and rocked to sleep by the movement of the bellows. Children were frequently despatched to Halesowen or Bromsgrove to collect the 60lb bundle of iron rods required for the week's work. Northfield specialised in the manufacture of large nails, and, using the simple equipment, it was possible for a young girl to turn out approximately 250 nails per hour. In 1960 Mrs Mabel White lived in one of the cottages, and although her mother had sung in Northfield church choir 100 years previously Mrs White did not inherit her good voice. Hers was said to resemble a 'Bumble Bee in a churn!' (P. Tidey-Hamilton)

Street Cottages were demolished in 1964 to make way for the construction of Great Stone Road. (J. Smith)

The old black and white temporary building opened in Bunbury Road in 1915 as Northfield Baptist church. Originally the road was called Bumbury Road. (*T. Hill*)

The busy scene today. Mrs E. Pickvance, who came to live in Bunbury Road in 1949, remembers walking along the road collecting wild flowers as she pushed the children in the pram. Later her children climbed trees and played in fields along the road prior to the building of the Ingoldsby estate which proceeded slowly but continuously in the immediate postwar years, when there were severe shortages of materials. A group of twelve houses was erected by contract in Bunbury Road before the Direct Works Department was reconstituted. (*J. Smith*)

The Grange and the Pigeon House. Seen here on the right of the photograph is the Pigeon House, which stood opposite the Grange at the top of Pigeon House Hill on the Bristol Road. It housed the servants and derived its name from the number of pigeons it accommodated to provide food for the residents of the Grange during the winter months. These made a welcome change to salted meat. A short underground passage led from the Pigeon House to the cellars of the Grange. For many years the Pigeon House was a private school, but when the tramline was extended to the Lickey Hills it gradually declined and in 1923 was demolished. During excavations in the early 1920s, following the demolition, sixteen Roman coins were found a hundred or so feet away, and the remains of an ancient aqueduct 15 feet below the surface. This ancient evidence of an artificial water supply was believed to be Roman work, but this idea has since been refuted. (*T. Hill*)

The entrance to Longbridge Social Club in 1970. The Grange, meaning a fortified farmhouse, was built in the late sixteenth century and was surrounded by a moat on three sides, the fourth side being protected by a sheer sandstone cliff. It was extended in the seventeenth century and farmed up to 1875 when it was then left unoccupied for ten years. After the turn of the twentieth century the house was bought and restored by a retired doctor who made extensive alterations to the grounds, turning a wilderness into beautiful gardens. While landscaping the garden two stone coffins were unearthed, one of which was used as a horse trough outside the Black Horse for many years. The Grange was used as a private hotel before being taken over in 1946 as Longbridge Social and Working Men's Club. (*O. Williams*)

Mill Lane took its name from the mill, which was on the corner of Mill Lane and Quarry Lane, and was known as both Northfield and Digbeth Mill. (*T. Hill*)

Mill Lane as it looks today. The houses look very much the same but the large trees have been felled and modern street lamps installed. (*J. Smith*)

Frankley Reservoir under construction. It was during the latter years of the nineteenth and early years of the twentieth centuries that Welsh water first came to Birmingham. The act authorising this was passed in 1892 and the mains laid four years later. Work was completed and the water came to Birmingham in 1904. (*S. Barnes*)

Frankley Reservoir today. The reservoir and filter beds on the Frankley/Northfield boundary store and purify this water. A new filter bed was opened early in 1954. (*J. Smith*)

This little railway, known as the Sand Line Train, was built in 1902 to take sand and stone from Hollyhill Quarry to the filter beds at the new reservoir at Frankley. There were three crossings on the line called New Street, Frogmill and Egghill. Mr P. Harding reports that an extract from Frankley Parish Council of 25 March 1901 states, 'When permission is given for the crossing at Egghill a crossing person must be in attendance'. Phil's great grandfather and great grandmother became the keepers, their duties being to open and close the crossing gates. They remained there until the line was closed a few years later. (*S. Barnes*)

Mrs Joyce Neave with Jennifer and Brenda, on Northfield Station in 1963. The local people welcomed the railway as affording easy access to Birmingham town. Miss Ryland, the owner of considerable property in the neighbourhood, gave three acres of land required for the site, and the Midland Railway Company, employing gangs of Irish navvies using brawn and shovel before the comforts of the mechanical aids of today, spent £4,000 on levelling the land, and erecting buildings and platforms. The rector records in the parish register that: 'The first train, conveying passengers

on the Birmingham to Gloucester Railway, passed through this Parish on 17 December 1840'. Homes for lower middle class people were erected nearby when the station was opened in 1869, and Woodland and Norman Roads were developed in the early twentieth century. Soon after the Second World War most farms and fields had been replaced by housing estates. (*J. Neave*)

3

Serving the Community

Jack Hunt and Jack Morris outside their house in Cock Lane, noted for the William pear tree growing up the side, which was always loaded with fruit. Cock Lane, later changed to Frankley Beeches Road, ran from the Black Horse pub on the Bristol Road up to the Cock Inn at Rubery. As well as being Captain of the Fire Brigade Jack Hunt knew a lot about animals and was used as the unofficial vet for the locality. Many people brought their animals to him for advice when they were unwell or injured. (*C. Read*)

Northfield fire crew around the turn of the nineteenth century. Until 1911, when Northfield became part of Birmingham, the fire brigade was a volunteer force. The original station was at 146, Maas Road, with the present one at the corner of South Road being built in 1959. (*C. Read*)

Among the crew members were Charlie Hodgetts, Harry Taylor, Sammy Stokes (the driver) and Jack Hunt (captain), who married Minnie Morris. (*C. Read*)

Jack Hunt, captain of the fire brigade. Until the building of the fire station in Mass Road, when not in use, the engine was kept in the garden of Jack and Minnie's house in Cock Lane. (*C. Read*)

The fire station and engines in 1998. The present fire station was built in 1959 at a cost of £48,281. It was to house two appliances with provision for an extension to take a third. On the ground floor were to be the fire offices, with the dormitory, mess rooms and kitchens on the first floor. In addition there was to be a hose tower and drill yards. It is presently being extended. (*R. de Boer*)

Photograph taken *c.*1920. Hearse and coaches outside the premises on the corner of Woodland Road and Church Hill where, around 1898, Mr Albert Morton started a funeral business. He was originally a local builder and cabinet maker who, when his mother-in-law died, decided to arrange her funeral. Other local people then asked him to arrange their family funerals, and the business grew from there. Mr Morton died in 1943 and his wife and family continued to run the business until their son Victor Morton came out of the RAF, when he took over. In 1950 he moved the business, now known as V. Morton & Sons, to its present premises in Bristol Road South. Vic, Ivy and their two sons, Grant and Miles, lived on the premises for approximately twenty years following the move. When it first began, funerals were few and far between, but it is not unusual today for Morton's to deal with ten on one day. (*V. Morton & Sons.*)

A hearse and limousine, one of Morton's latest fleet, in Northfield Road, 2001. (*V. Morton & Sons.*)

Mr Albert Morton and family on the steps of their home in Church Hill in the early 1900s.
(*V. Morton & Sons.*)

This double-decker bus, outside Smoky Joes in 1966, was used by Andy's Coaches as a staff bus to transport workers to the Austin Motor Works. It was an ex-public transport bus based at Brighton and belonging to Southdown Motor Services. (*R. de Boer*)

Two D9 type Midland Red buses outside the gas showroom in 1970. These were 144-service buses, which went from Birmingham, through Worcester and on to Great Malvern. Note the passengers about to board the rear bus having been transferred from the bus in front, which has broken down. (*R. de Boer*)

De-regulation allowed private bus operation on public routes. This Patterson's Bus, photographed on Church Road in 1993, ran from Northfield to Bournville and out to the QE Hospital. (*R. de Boer*)

The Budget Bus, seen here in 1996, on Bristol Road South, ran from Northfield to Frankley shopping centre. Following de-regulation a number of operators, including Pattersons, Budget, Pete's Travel, Zak's and West Midlands Travel have run services, for a while, around the Northfield area. (*R. de Boer*)

The Co-operative Butchers, which was said to sell the best fresh meat in Northfield, was on the site of the Bell Inn on the corner of Bristol Road South and Bell Lane. Mrs Sansom tells us her husband Arthur is the apprentice on the right of the photograph. (*Mrs H.J. Sansom*)

A photograph taken in March 1965 of Walter J. Sylvester making dough in the bakehouse owned by Dennis Overton in Bell Lane. Walter began life as a baker with Roy's Bakery in Bournville. From there he moved to Mary Ford's in Raddlebarn Road, Jewells of Stirchley, renowned for their top quality pork pies, and then on to the bakery in Bell Lane. (*I. Sylvester*)

An Austin 301, descendant of Loadstar, belonging to Ten Acres and Stirchley Co-Operative Society (TASCOS), whose identity ceased in 1971. The lorry brought crates of one third of a pint milk bottles to St Laurence CE Schools in winter in the 1950s. The milk was warmed on the coke-filled boilers prior to the pupils drinking it. It also doubled as a coal lorry! Photograph taken in the 1980s of the lorry then derelict in Shropshire. (*W. Staniforth*)

Photographed in 1972 in Bunbury Road, this van began life as a laundry van but as more people acquired washing machines, and commercial laundries became less viable, it was converted into a fruit van and later became a hot dog van frequently seen serving customers on Tay's corner. (*R. de Boer*)

Photograph taken *c.* 1948. The Longbridge Laundry was at the bottom of Mill Lane. It advertised as 'High Class Launderers, Dyers and Dry Cleaners', stating that 'A post card will bring our van or, if you prefer, any of the following local agents will receive work for us'. Agents were listed in West Heath, Northfield and Kings Norton. (*R de Boer*)

Charles Brown outside Cofton Common Farm. Sarah Wheale, who married William Brown, was born at 6, Church Hill. William died in the great 'flu epidemic of 1918. One of their family, Arthur, bought Ash Bank Farm on Bristol Road. He had five children – Charles (pictured), Jack, Joyce, Ben and Spencer. They each had a milk round and were a familiar sight throughout the village. (*T. Hill*)

This small petrol filling station on Bristol Road South, photographed in 1975 and affectionately known as Dirty Dicks, was owned by Archibald Hodges. Just down from The Black Horse it was known as the Alpha Works and from 1925–46 the site also acted as a depot for the mineral water manufacturers Apollinaris Co. Ltd. Art Hodges recalls that during the war there was an open workshop with a shelf along the sides at which ladies sat painting hand grenades. It is now a car spare parts outlet. (*R. de Boer*)

Milk floats queuing up along the Bristol Road to enter the dairy in the mid-1970s. The depot was too small for the larger Morrisons vehicles so five-wheeled vehicles were used. Midland Counties Dairy was later taken over by Unigate who had 32 milk rounds around Northfield. Some floats were made of fibreglass and some metal, but all received heavy treatment, and it was not at all unusual to see floats on the road with panels missing. The dairy was closed down in 1981. (*R de Boer*)

A tram coming up the Bristol Road hill by the Woodlands Hospital. Apart from a few privately owned bus services, public transport by road in Birmingham really commenced with the tramway era in the 1870s, but it was not until 1904 that the Corporation began to operate its own services. In 1919 The Corporation Tramways Act authorised the extension of the tram services along the Bristol Road. In the early 1920s the tramway system was extended from Selly Oak to Northfield then on to Longbridge in December 1923 and to Rednal in April 1924. As the tramway routes became unremunerative, they were

replaced by motorbus services, the first change taking place in 1930 and the whole programme being completed by 4 July 1953. Along the Bristol Road buses completely replaced the trams on 6 July 1952. (*T. Hill*)

Mr Robert C. Saunders writes:

In 1952 I was a young serving Police Officer based at Selly Oak and later at Longbridge, when I was posted to duty as security on the last tram from Birmingham to Cotteridge and from Northfield to Selly Oak. The tram to Cotteridge contained most of the civic dignitaries from Birmingham including the town clerk and I think the Lord Mayor. On arrival at Cotteridge we were all transferred to a single decker bus and transported to Northfield where the last tram to Selly Oak was waiting for us. My most lasting memory is of the crowds of people lining the whole route from Birmingham to Selly Oak in a well behaved and carnival type atmosphere. It was a wonderful experience.

William Hodge's (Art's grandfather) Humber, *c.* 1920 – a two-seater with a 'Dickie'. Walter, William and Alfred Hodge worked for William (Snr)'s Company known as Hodge Brothers which had a yard in Frankley Beeches Road. They did contract work for the Public Works Department and travelled all over the country, one of them having to use the 'Dickie' seat in the rear, which was open to the elements, in all weathers. Part of their work was installing the pipes from the Elan Valley to the reservoir at Frankley. In this photograph Art is in the 'Dickie' seat with Chris (his cousin) in the driving seat and Bobby Brewer in the front. (*A. Hodge*)

Agnes Buckley (née) Wilkes lived in a cottage, which had gargoyles under the eaves, on the corner of Turves Green and West Heath Roads, Northfield. Her granddaughter, Pam Hambidge, remembers her grandparents owning many animals. She helped her grandad plant potatoes in his garden, pick pears off the tree on the wall of the house, and apples which were stored in baskets in the second room which had been the old nail shop from where nails were made and sold. The cottage contained a single living/dining-room with a large fire in a black lead grate with hooks in the chimney to smoke meat and ovens either side in which to cook. The room seemed very small to bring up a family of six children, but all thrived. The back kitchen contained a large, low sink and a heavy wooden mangle. (*P. Hambidge*)

The Hodge family taken at 22, Cock Lane, which was their home until the family increased sufficiently to warrant building a new home. Art is the boy in the sailor suit who is about three years old, together with his mother and two sisters, Dolly and Ivy. Art's father and his two brothers, Walter, William and Alfred, paid for The Sons of Rest building in Victoria Common, which was officially opened by his grandmother. They also financed the cinemas at Northfield, Rubery and Weoley Castle. (*A. Hodge*)

The Morris family of Digbeth Mill in the early 1900s. Left to right, back row: Percy, Maud, Wally, Ada. Middle row: 'Grandma' Morris, Minnie. Front row: Amy, Jack. (*C. Read*)

Mary Banton with her parents, *c.* 1930. Mr and Mrs B. Banton were both active and well known in the village, Mr Banton being a church warden for several years as well as being involved in other activities. Mrs Banton belonged to many organisations, and was enrolling member of the Mothers Union in the 1930s, 40s and 50s. Mary and her sister Jean were closely involved with the Guides and Rangers. (*M. Banton*)

Ready for all emergencies! The Bantons' garden in Woodland Road, *c.* 1941. Jean Banton is on the right, wearing a posh leather gas mask carrier, and with padded shoulders, as was the fashion in the early 1940s, and Mrs B. Banton is in the middle with her sister from Lugwardine on the left. (*M. Banton*)

An Anderson shelter pictured in 1980 in a garden at the rear of Roger de Boer's home in Bristol Road South. Following the war years the shelter was used as a larder, and was finally demolished in 1990. (*R. de Boer*)

P₂ 441682

The Statutory Fee for this Certificate is 2s. 7d. If required subsequently to registration, a Search Fee is payable in addition.

CERTIFIED COPY of an **ENTRY OF MARRIAGE.**
Pursuant to the Marriage **Acts, 1811 to 1934.**

Registration District *Birmingham*

1937. Marriage Solemnized at *The Parish Church*
of *Northfield* in the *County Borough of Birmingham*

Columns:— 1	2	3	4	5	6	
No. When Married.	Name and Surname.	Age.	Condition.	Rank or Profession.	Residence at the time of Marriage.	Fa
243 27² December 1937	John Laister	25	Bachelor	Motor Engineer	5 Berwick Grove Northfield	Will
	Hilda Tidey-Hamilton	33	Widow	—	5 Berwick Grove Northfield	Ja

Married in the *Parish Church* according to the Rites and Ceremonies of the *Established Church* by

This Marriage was solemnized between us, { *John Laister* / *Hilda Tidey-Hamilton* } in the Presence of us, { *Alban William Price* / *Francis Henry Thomas* }

I, *Reginald Andrew Haygon*, Rector of *Northfield* in the *County Boro* a true copy of the Entry No. *243*, in the Register Book of Marriages of the said Church.

WITNESS MY HAND this 27² day of *December* 19*37*.

CAUTION.—Any person who (1) falsifies any of the particulars on this Certificate, or (2) uses it as true, knowing it to be falsified, is liable to Prosecution.

John and Hilda Laister on their Golden Wedding Day in 1987. They never looked back and enjoyed fifty-one-and-a-half wonderfully happy years together. During the Second World War John was in the Austin Home Guard. (*J. Laister*)

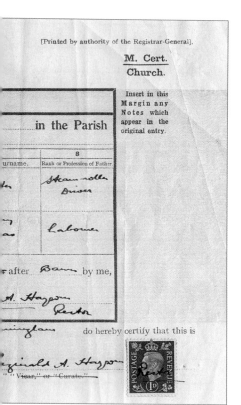

John Laister's Marriage Certificate. John came to Birmingham from the North in November 1936 for an interview at the Austin Motor Company. He stayed overnight with Hilda Tidey-Hamilton, a widow with an eight-year-old daughter, Pat. Following his interview John returned home but could not get Hilda and Pat out of his mind and felt they needed someone to look after them, so he sent a telegram saying, 'Coming tomorrow'. He duly returned and he and Hilda were married on 27 December 1937, at St Laurence Church following a two-inch snowfall. Money was very short, and it cost ten shillings (a tidy sum in those days) for one car to do two trips, one taking Hilda's mother and father to the church, the other bringing Hilda, John and Pat back. Therefore, to save further expense John, Hilda and Pat walked to the church from their home in Berwick Grove. (*J. Laister*)

The parish church of St Laurence. It is believed that monks who came from Dudley Priory about the year 1000 AD built the first church at Northfield. There was certainly a sizeable Norman church in the twelfth century, approximating the present church in size. Records show that pictures painted on the walls inside the church were washed out in 1650 following the royal injunction to remove all pictures, crosses and the like from church buildings. The early buildings were replaced in the late Middle Ages, the south aisle and porch in the fourteenth century, and the top stage of the tower in the fifteenth century. The north aisle was built in the nineteenth century and the vestries in the mid-twentieth century. The lych gate was built in 1863, and the fourteenth-century timbered porch is built entirely of oak and has enclosed sides with a plain bargeboard. Thus the present church represents a variety of architectural styles throughout the ages. (*D. Mayo*)

Karen and Trudi Smith in the play area, Victoria Common in 1963. Victoria Common, first opened to the public in 1897, was formerly known as Bradley Field, and was one of the village's great open fields, where villagers each held strips of land divided by deep furrows, the remnants of which give the corrugated effect, called 'ridge and furrow', still seen on the present day turfed surface. Note the paving stones here in the children's play area. Bark chippings followed these, but the play area has now been moved to a new site and a special soft-fall surface laid under the equipment. Half a million pounds from the Northfield Regeneration fund is to be spent on refurbishing the tennis courts, football pitches and bowling green on the Common, and a brand new all-weather pitch will provide opportunities for a variety of sports, such as basketball, netball and soccer. (*J. Smith*)

The new play area on Victoria Common. It was recently reported in the *Birmingham Evening Mail* that, following a report from the Royal Society for the Prevention of Accidents, which discovered that swings in certain older play areas did not meet recently introduced European guidelines, the City Council decided to spend £100,000 upgrading equipment and installing special safety surfaces in forty-four Birmingham playgrounds, to bring them up to the required standard. (*J. Smith*)

4

Schools

8th June, 1946

TO-DAY, AS WE CELEBRATE VICTORY, I send this personal message to you and all other boys and girls at school. For you have shared in the hardships and dangers of a total war and you have shared no less in the triumph of the Allied Nations.

I know you will always feel proud to belong to a country which was capable of such supreme effort; proud, too, of parents and elder brothers and sisters who by their courage, endurance and enterprise brought victory. May these qualities be yours as you grow up and join in the common effort to establish among the nations of the world unity and peace.

George R.I.

A certificate sent to all children who attended school throughout the years of the Second World War. This one was kindly loaned by Mrs Margaret Bearman. (*M. Bearman*)

Northfield School. In May 1714 Dr William Worth, the Rector of Northfield, ordered some books and began his new charity school with twenty boys. By 1834 it became obvious that another school was needed and the building pictured was erected in 1837 at a cost of £288 of which £100 was a grant from the National Society and the rest parishioners' contributions. This was a one-roomed school with an adjoining schoolmaster's house, which served as a Sunday School where children of the parish could learn the three R's. (During the week even

children as young as seven or eight were doing a full day's work.) In 1844 the new school amalgamated with the charity school as a day school, any child being able to attend on payment of a small fee, ranging from 1*d* to 6*d* per week. However, this still precluded children from the poorest families. By 1850 there were seventy pupils taught by one headmaster with an assistant mistress and two monitors. The central part is the old school, but because of the rapidly increasing numbers additions were made at intervals throughout the nineteenth century. Note the pointed windows with small panes set in cast-iron frames, and the scalloped and fretted bargeboards denoting very typical architecture of the Victorian period. (*D. Mayo*)

St Laurence CE Schools, 1978. By 1870 there were 114 children divided into two schools – boys and girls, but the numbers continued to increase so rapidly that in 1898 the girls were given separate premises in a new building. Although the old school held affectionate memories for many in the parish, the trials of those who had to work in it were tremendous. There were seven fires to light each morning. Flooded classrooms and ceilings coming down were quite normal events. When it rained heavily doors at the front and back had to be

opened to sweep the water out, and in winter it became so cold the ink froze in the inkwells – not to mention the dreadful outside toilets! With the advent of North Sea Gas only a miracle saved the school from an explosion in the very old pipes. Eventually increasing numbers and deteriorating conditions led to both schools moving to new sites and the 'Old School' was vacated. (*R. de Boer*)

St Laurence School's Ryland House, in a state of dereliction, 1974. The house was given to the school by the Ryland family, local benefactors, for use as a dwelling for the headteacher. The Revd Peter Penny occupied it during his time as headmaster, but Mrs Barbara Davis, not wishing to live there, requested that the house be given to the school for use as a teaching area. It was turned into a 'Little House of Numbers' using a different aspect of maths in each part of the house.

Posters were displayed with all the essential words for maths and the stairs were used to learn ordinal numbers going one way and cardinal the other. Mrs Davis implemented a project of estimation for certain activities, e.g. weighing and measuring, which taught the children not to be afraid of admitting 'I Was Wrong', when the outcome was incorrect. Ryland House became highly regarded over a very wide area and many inspectors made a special visit to the school to see it. (*R. de Boer*)

The new St Laurence Junior School. It was in 1946 that the Revd J. Crowle Ellis launched an appeal for the cost of rebuilding the schools as a Voluntary Aided Junior and Infant School, at an estimated cost to the managers of £18,000. Later the managers were asked to increase the size, and to divide the school into separate Junior and Infant Departments, the division coming on 1

January 1964. The changes meant additional buildings, increasing the expected cost to the managers to £42,000. Authority was not given for any building until 1956–7 and then only for four classrooms of the Junior School as it was over-flowing into the Church Hall and Northfield Institute. Because of difficulties with a grant from the Ministry of Education, in 1952 the managers contributed to the Diocese of Birmingham Aided Schools Fund, a scheme designed to enable voluntary aided schools in the Diocese to spread the cost of new buildings over twenty to twenty-five years by the payment of annual premiums. However, in 1956, when the Fund was still in its infancy, the managers decided to fund the building of the four classrooms, which were erected in 1958, without calling on the Fund. The remainder of the school was authorized in 1961–2 under the Local Authority Development Programme, and the new Junior School, standing in its own grounds and with its own sports field, was officially dedicated and opened on 6 June 1964. (*J. Smith*)

The new St Laurence Infant School. In November 1972 the Infant School moved to the same site as the Junior School leaving the 1837 buildings on Church Hill, which had become virtually unusable. It accommodated 360 children in nine light and airy classrooms with a hall and its own kitchen overlooking the park in front and the school playing fields at the back. (*J. Smith*)

The new St Laurence Infant School was dedicated and opened by the Bishop of Birmingham on 7 July 1973. Left to right, Mr H.W.W. Gumbley (Diocesan Representative), Mrs Barbara Davis (headteacher), The Rt Revd Bishop Brown, Bishop of Birmingham, The Ven. Vernon Nicholls, Archdeacon of Birmingham, Mrs E.M. Canaway (Parochial Church Council Representative), -?-, Councillor H.N. Scrimshaw (Local Education Authority Representative). (*B. Davis*)

Staff at the St Laurence CE 'Old' School in the late 1960s photographed in front of Ryland House. Back row, left to right: Student, Mrs D. Kestle, Mrs D. Harvey, Mrs D.I. Laugharne, Mrs P. Radford. Front row: Mrs W. Ellis, Mrs O. Kimberley, Mrs J. Rice (deputy headteacher), Mrs B. Davis (headteacher), Mrs J. Gross, Mrs D. Chandler, Shaun Chandler and Mrs J. Ludlam. (*B. Davis*)

Children from St Laurence Infant School were invited to help promote the annual Poppy Appeal, launched in the terrace restaurant at the Bournville Factory of Cadbury Ltd in October 1984. Victoria Watson sang *The Poppy Song* which she had composed for the Royal British Legion. (*J. Smith*)

Standard IV, Northfield School (later St Laurence CE School), 17 October 1932. (*O. Williams*)

Mr John Andrews' class of boys and girls from St Laurence 'Old' School in 1957. Joyce Brown's cottage can be seen in the background. (*J. Andrews*)

A Nativity play performed by Mrs Ellis' reception class at the 'Old' St Laurence Infant School in 1970. (*A. Courbet*)

A pageant at St Laurence Infant School in 1976. (*A. Courbet*)

A view of St Laurence 'Old' School in 1971 from Pamela Road looking up Church Hill. Following closure of the 'Old' School the Northfield Society, which began as a conservation group to save the 'Old' School, campaigned for a preservation order to be placed on the buildings thus saving them from demolition. (*R. de Boer*)

The same view today. The site was sold and the buildings restored and converted into a number of private dwellings. The character has been retained; window lights have been installed in the roof and the double doors in the centre of the two buildings removed. Roger de Boer recalls when he was door monitor he was given a 'Lollipop' to put across the double doors to prevent children leaving. (*J. Smith*)

Nativity play at Frankley Beeches Day Nursery in 1949. Like many other day nurseries Frankley Beeches was opened by the Corporation in the early 1940s to look after children in order to free their mothers for war work. The youngsters were taken in from the age of six weeks to five years, and placed into three groups: Babies – six to twelve months, Tweenies – twelve months to two-and-a-half years and Toddlers – two-and-a-half to five years. It was fully staffed with a Matron, Sister, nurses, and assistant nurses, and during the war years was open six days a week from 7a.m.–8p.m. (G. Wilkins)

Tea at the Christmas party at Frankley Beeches Day Nursery in 1949. The parents had to pay a fee for the children to attend, but they were very well looked after. The first duty of the staff was to bath them and change them into nursery clothes. They then laundered all the clothes they had removed from the children. Gladys Wilkins began work there when she was fourteen years old and stayed for approximately eight years. She remembers it as very hard, but rewarding work. The nursery eventually closed around 1953 and was then pulled down. (G. Wilkins)

In 1925 this house, number 1211, Bristol Road South, was called The Meadows and was lived in by Edward and Esther Harper who had one daughter. Mrs C. Read, who was a friend of the daughter, recalls attending functions in the grounds before the Second World War. It later seems to have had a varied and changeable life as records show that by 1946 the occupant was a Mr Roy Mountford and the house had become the Bethany Maternity and Nursing Home, the proprietor being Mrs E. Mountford. (Mrs Wendy Morgan (Secretary at the Meadows School) recalls her brother Paul Smith, a recipient of the CBSO long

service award, being born there in 1947.) By 1948 the name had changed again to Northfield Maternity Nursing Home with the proprietresses a Mrs Joan Beasley and Mrs Alice E.S. George. In 1949–55 it is registered as H.E. Brookes Building Con. and Wm Moorman Rt. Hostel. 1956–63 shows Mrs L.M. Moorman – Private Hotel: 1964–6 Mrs L.M. Moorman – Apartments, and 1967 the Meadows School. (*The Meadows School*)

The Meadows School, which was built on land adjacent to where the house stood and took the name of the house, opened on 5 November 1957. By January 1958 the school had eighty-two children on the role. Today it has 450 pupils including those in the Language Unit. The school has a challenging atmosphere where purposeful learning takes place in a large, well-equipped building. It also has two small classes for children with formal Statements of Special Educational Needs for speech and language disorders where there are two

teachers, two nursery nurses and a full time speech therapist who work with the children. Two teachers support children integrating them into mainstream classes. Children gradually increase the amount of integration with mainstream classes in preparation for a return to their local school. There is the benefit of additional teacher support when unit and mainstream children work together. (*The Meadows School*)

A day visit in term time by children from the Meadows School to No. 10 Downing Street. (*The Meadows School*)

A primary school recorder group at the Meadows School in 1984. (*The Meadows School*)

Mr H.W.J. Green, Bellfield School's first headteacher, recalls his first visit to the site on which the school was to be built – Bell Hill, a large field containing a pond and perched on a hill. The field was where the stage-coach horses, which stopped at the Old Bell Inn, had been rested; therefore the name Bellfield seemed appropriate for the school. Bellfield Junior and Infant Schools were built to provide accommodation for children formerly in attendance at the Junior and Infant Departments of Tinkers Farm Primary School in order to free the whole of the accommodation at Tinkers Farm for secondary

OFFICIAL OPENING BY
THE RT. HON. THE EARL ATTLEE, K.G., P.C., O.M., C.H.
ON TUESDAY, 15TH OCTOBER 1957
AT 10.30 A.M.

school use. This became necessary to meet the increasing demand for such accommodation arising mainly from housing developments in the vicinity. The closure of the Tinkers Farm Primary School and the transfer of staff and pupils to the new Bellfield Schools took place following the 1957 Whitsun holidays, and The Right Honourable The Earl Attlee officially opened the schools on Tuesday 15 October 1957. (*H.W.J. Green*)

Bellfield School, Infant Reception Class. Mr Green particularly liked the non-cloakroom plan – wide corridors with permanent seats all the way along and fixed far enough out from the walls for coats to hang behind. He remembers he arrived just in time to have the toilet fittings in the first year block installed in suitable sizes and levels for seven-year olds' use, though he also remembers one disaster. To economise on material it was decided to abandon upstairs toilets in the main block and double the size of the

accommodation on the ground floor. The main assembly hall had supplementary heated-air machines for use in winter and the newly planned boys' toilets were built across the air intakes. Imagine the smells heated up and pumped at pressure into morning assembly! The system had a very short life. Bellfield was one of only two schools in the country to integrate deaf children with hearing children. (*H.W.J. Green*)

During Mr Green's headship the school presented a yearly opera and in 1961 the *Bromsgrove Messenger* reported that 'an unusually attractive show, *There and Back Again* was presented by Bellfield Junior School, Northfield with a large cast of boys and girls whose ages ranged from seven to eleven years. H.W.J. Green, the headmaster, wrote the book and music which deals with a mix-up of nursery rhymes interrupted by a gang of Teddy Boys and Beatniks, who intrude on to the pages of the children's book. The action took place within a dream and started with Tom the Piper's son stealing the pig of the Farmer at the unusual rendezvous of the Old Woman's Shoe'. (*H.W.J. Green*)

Another Bellfield School opera taking place in the South Sea Islands. (*H.W.J. Green*)

Longwill School under construction on Bell Hill in 1962. A 'three-in-one' school campus, which included some of the most modern equipment and facilities to help and test handicapped children, was opened on 21 April 1964 at Bell Holloway, Northfield. The campus brought together three special day schools each founded near the city centre between 1895 and 1929 – the Victoria School for the physically handicapped, the Longwill School for deaf and partially deaf

children and the George Auden School for the partially sighted. Though in separate buildings they shared many communal facilities. At the opening Mr H.M. Cohen said 'there have been many advances in medical science and in physics and only by setting up new buildings are we able to take advantage of new developments'. The campus began with 130 physically handicapped, 120 deaf and partially deaf and 50 partially sighted pupils. The schools cater for children from all over South Birmingham and neighbouring parts of Worcestershire and Warwickshire, but the George Auden School has since closed. (*Longwill School*)

An etching of Longwill School when the building was completed. Longwill School, which began as Moseley Road School for deaf children in 1895, takes children from the ages of two-and-a-half to sixteen and above. In the nursery unit, besides ordinary nursery school activities, they are given, at what is probably the most vital age of all, special training in the use of hearing aids and in the

beginnings of speech. To develop the fullest use of each child's residual hearing, the school was equipped with the latest group hearing aid and inductance loop systems. Classes are small so that individual attention may be given to the acquisition of language. The school has worked closely with the audiological centre at the Birmingham Children's Hospital and co-operated in the training of teachers with the Department of Audiology and Education of the Deaf of the University of Manchester. It has specialist rooms and equipment and aims at a wide, active and varied education. (*Longwill School*)

The Victoria School provides special help for physically handicapped children aged between three and sixteen. Some handicaps are congenital and some the result of illness or accident. As well as teachers, the school has its own physiotherapists, nurses and attendants. Visiting speech therapists work in teams to give each child as full and normal a school life as he or she can have. In this, art and music, swimming and drama are all important activities. (*Victoria School*)

A class working at Victoria School *c.* 1964. (*Victoria School*)

Trescott School, here photographed in 2001, is built 15 minutes' walk away from Frankley Beeches, a plantation of beech trees 830 ft above sea level, which overlooks Frankley Reservoir. The school opened with 340 children under the headship of Miss Cotterell on 24 August 1931. It is a veranda type school with all

classrooms opening on both sides with doors onto a large open asphalt playground. At that time the majority of parents of attendees worked at the Austin Motor Works. In 1944 owing to the close co-operation between home and school during the war years due to the evacuation, and the opening of a nursery and play centre it was decided to form a PTA. The membership fee started at 3d and the following year rose to 1s to cover the cost of programme printing. Surplus funds were used to provide vases for the hall and a donation was given towards a sunray lamp for use in the nursery. (*J. Smith*)

A class at Trescott School in 1931, the opening year of the school. In 1941 there was a great drive for women in industry and as the school is near the Austin Motor Works mothers asked if they could bring their children aged under five years old to the school. A first nursery class was formed in December of that year, and in a few months numbers had grown sufficiently to warrant a second class being formed. In August 1942 there was need for a third class, so, at the suggestion of inspectors, the nurseries moved from wooden huts to the main building and became a self-contained nursery. (*Trescott School*)

A physical training display, which was part of the programme for a parents' day at Trescott Junior Mixed School, 18 July 1951. Addressing a large audience the headmistress said that the most remarkable feature of the year had been the tremendous growth in numbers. There were now over a hundred more in the school than during the Christmas term, children from Rednal and Turves Green having been directed to Trescott Road. (*Trescott School*)

Boys during a handwork lesson at Trescott School preparing a display called 'Ships Through The Ages' for the end of term open evening in the summer of 1961. (*Trescott School*)

St Brigid's RC School was the first new school to be opened in the Archdiocese after the war, being blessed and formally opened by Archbishop Masterson on 21 July 1951. The close alliance between church and Catholic school is one of the most enriching elements of St Brigid's parish life. Unlike many other Catholic primary schools all the heads to the  present day have been religious sisters. From 1973 the numbers of children and teachers dropped rapidly so much so that by the 1980s in many parts of the country it was difficult to keep Catholic schools going. However, despite ever greater government pressures, St Brigid's continued to flourish, growing in faith and the formation of young children. The pre-school group started in 1982 and was so well run that it was one of the very few in Birmingham allowed to make the transition to fully established nursery school status. (*St Brigid's School*)

A class working at St Brigid's School in 1950. Note the double desks with opening lids and well for the storage of books, and the inkwells and pen and pencil indentations on the surface. Through the right-hand window an Anderson shelter can be seen. In July 1984 St Brigid's School was selected to join the BBC's Anniversary Festivities at Pebble Mill, where they participated in workshops related to country dancing and introducing science. The host on the day of their visit was the Olympic swimmer Duncan Goodhew. (*St Brigid's School*)

Children from St Brigid's School all prepared for a coach outing in the days when girls wore berets and boys wore caps. (*St Brigid's School*)

St Brigid's School pupils working out in the community in 1998–9 where they have planted new trees on Manor Farm Park and in Frankley Beeches Road. (*St Brigid's School*)

Tinker's Farm Senior Mixed Council School opened in huts in August 1931, on what became known as the Tinkers Farm estate. The name refers to tinkers who lived on a farm near the village of Northfield and who mended kettles and pans and manufactured horseshoes and nails, though the farm is said to have originally been owned by Colonel 'Tinker' Fox, renowned for his exploits in this area during the Civil War. The school was erected on the site of the old farmhouse,

which was built at the end of the seventeenth century, three storeys high, moated and latterly haunted. The first headmistress, Miss H.R. Walmesley, once told of a walk from Selly Oak to the Lickey Hills during which she came across some men cutting down an apple orchard. They told her that a school was to be built but little did she think that it was the school to which she would later come as headmistress. In 1933 the school split into separate single sex departments, the girls occupying the upper floors while the boys' were in the lower part. It remained that way until re-organised to form Northfield Comprehensive School in 1969. (*Beazer Partnerships Midlands*)

The 'Dig for Victory' campaign, photographed here in 1942–3, was followed in the school, the garden between the senior and infant buildings being adapted for agricultural use. The playing fields were also ploughed and used for crops, and during the autumn term, up to eighty boys helped lift potatoes on local farms. At the outbreak of war the schools were closed while essential work was carried out to the buildings and shelters erected. They re-opened on a part-time voluntary basis, and compulsory attendance was re-introduced on 22 January 1940. The shelters were first used in August 1940 when the log book records, 'air-raid warning during assembly. Plane heard, guns fired'. On 13 November 1940 there were two raids during school hours during which time there was a hit on the Austin Motor Works. (*M. Valente*)

Northfield Comprehensive School became Northfield School in 1974, and closed in July 1986 when the buildings were taken over by community groups. In June 2000 the buildings were demolished and the site is now being developed as a housing estate. When it opened the building was a showpiece attracting visits from educationalists from all over the world. The school was open-plan, the classroom walls being the outer walls of the building and pupils lined up in the playground to enter the downstairs classrooms. Many classrooms had sliding 'walls' which were hinged and could be folded back on sunny days. The emphasis was always on fresh air. (*Beazer Partnerships Midlands*)

Honeycombe Way on Scholars Green, the housing estate now being erected by Beazer Partnerships Midlands on the site where Tinkers Farm/Northfield School once stood. (*J. Smith*)

The authors' aunt, Miss C.E. Jones, was headmistress of the Woodlands Hospital School from 1950 until her retirement in December 1968. When she began work there the school had four wards and most patients were polio or TB sufferers nursed in open-air wards with purely a roof to shelter them from the elements, fresh air in those days being considered the cure for all ills! Tarpaulins were provided to cover the beds in severe weather (we have heard her talk about piles of snow collecting on the foot of the beds on several occasions) when staff, working in spartan conditions donned mackintoshes, coats, woolly scarves, hats and gloves, warm leggings and boots in order to keep the school running. As the number of polio and TB admissions declined they were followed by accident and spinal cases, moving into general orthopaedics as surgery advanced and, to the delight of the staff, into closed wards! In addition to her work at the Woodlands, Miss Jones was also head of the school at the Forelands Convalescent Hospital near Bromsgrove, and travelled there twice a week until its closure and amalgamation with the Woodlands when she was instrumental in the inception and setting up of Ward 11. (*J. Smith*)

Mrs Lavinia Fellows (extreme right), present headteacher of Woodlands Hospital School, with members of her staff, Christmas 1995. The Woodlands, the oldest hospital school in Birmingham and the second oldest hospital school in the country, commenced on 1 May 1914 and from that time it has been necessary for staff to learn to cope with the changing patterns of disease and the tremendous strides made in medical and surgical understanding. In 1948 the Birmingham Education Committee assumed financial responsibility for the school together with the powers of appointment and dismissal of teachers. In January 1957

because of low numbers, particularly among the girls, one teacher was lost from the staff. By 1985 the character of the school was altered so much regarding length and type of admission that the best way of deploying staff needed urgent consideration, and Governors were informed that two teachers would need to be redeployed because of falling rolls. Today, patients mostly have short, but in many cases, numerous admissions to the hospital and the school is reduced to one ward. (*Woodlands Hospital School*)

Ward 11, the Royal Orthopaedic Hospital. By 1973 all children were to be admitted on to Ward 11. In 1965 the school at the Forelands Convalescent Hospital in Bromsgrove ceased to exist as a separate school and became part of the Woodlands Hospital School. In the 1970s the Woodlands Hospital

School took under its wing the Regional Adolescent Psychiatric Unit at Hollymoor Hospital thus making it a two-site school with a great contrast between the teaching requirements of the Orthopaedic pupils and the often over-active Psychiatric ones. In 1989 Computer Aided Learning was added to the curriculum. On 20 May 1996 a meeting took place to discuss proposals for the setting up of a Unified Hospital School to include the Tuition Service, and the Secretary of State for Education approved the closure of the Woodlands Hospital School with effect from 31 August 1996. The Unified School was a major landmark for all types of hospital school provision in the city. The last day of the Woodlands Hospital School was on 19 July 1996, the school having existed for eighty-two years. It then came under the umbrella of the James Brindley School, which covers ten sites across the city of Birmingham as well as home teaching for children with special needs living within the city boundaries. (*Woodlands Hospital School*)

Just like any other school corridors those surrounding Ward 11 are beautifully decorated with the children's schoolwork.

Notes from the School Log Books. 'On 25 October 1926 two teachers were reported absent and the cold wind in the wards over the previous few days was reported as being intense, resulting in severe colds amongst patients and staff'. 'On the night of 22/23 November 1940 a hit was made on the hospital by enemy air force resulting in a direct hit on the Committee Room. The headteacher's desk, together with all its contents, was completely buried under the debris. Four attendance and two admission registers were the only books salvaged and in a battered condition.' (*Woodlands Hospital School*)

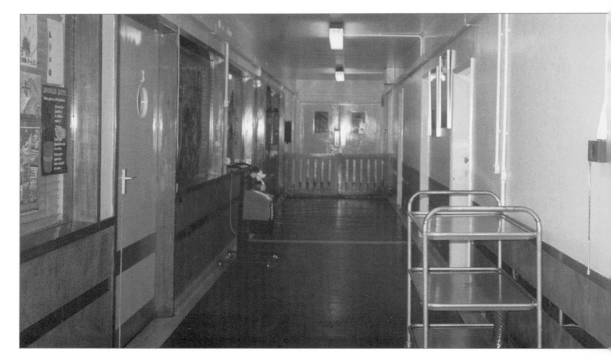

In 1995 Sister Maggie Nendick (Sister on Ward 11) at the Royal Orthopaedic Hospital, decided that the corridor leading directly to the ward was rather dull and uninteresting, so she commissioned the daughter of the present headteacher, Katherine Fellows, and her friend Jenny Kruger, to paint a mural to brighten it up. (*Woodlands Hospital School*)

The two girls, who were students at the University of Stoke-on-Trent Faculty of Art, painted the mural in their spare time, and the League of Friends of the Hospital provided funds for their materials. In May 2001 the Birmingham Evening Mail reported that the Cabinet Office Minister Ian McCartney recently visited and highly praised the work of the James Brindley Hospital School. He said there were similar hospital teaching schemes in Britain but nothing on the scale of Birmingham. An appeal has now been launched for £1.5 million to build a new Child Assessment Centre. (*Woodlands Hospital School*)

The egg collection group in the early 1950s. An annually-organised event from the Northfield Village Institute, this was to encourage children to collect eggs for use at the 'Royal Cripples' Hospital', now the Royal Orthopaedic Hospital. After collection a large crocodile of children, carrying tin baths, washing baskets, and any container that would carry the eggs safely, processed steadily down the Bristol Road to the hospital where they were warmly received by the patients. The Matron in the photograph is Miss Mountain. (*S. Bowden*)

A certificate was always awarded to the person collecting the most eggs. This certificate was awarded to Janet Upton (née Priestnall) in 1951. (*J. Upton*)

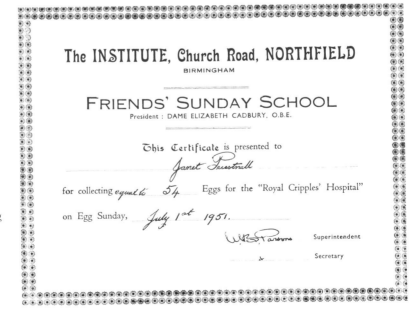

Ley Hill JI (NC) School in the early 1960s. Ley Hill School was built in 1954 on a hillside of meadowland where cattle grazed. The school opened with ninety children on the roll, which increased to 600 within three years. This necessitated the erection of additional school buildings, and an estate with houses and high-rise flats quickly grew up around it. (*P. Tidey-Hamilton*)

Ley Hill School in 2001. Visually the school is little changed but note the flats in the background. At present the estate is being cleared on a phased programme. Many residents have already been re-housed, and the flats are soon to be demolished. A team of architects is currently doing surveys, meeting with agencies, local residents and young people to develop a plan for the future look of the estate. Many families who enjoy living on Ley Hill want to stay, and are keen to work with the City Council to develop new housing, community facilities and services that will make Ley Hill a pleasant place to live. (*J. Smith*)

5

Leisure Time

Dick Spooner, left, and 'Tiger' Smith, 1951. E.J. 'Tiger' Smith was born in Highgate, Birmingham in 1886, the year the Edgbaston Cricket Ground was officially opened. He joined the Warwickshire playing staff in 1904 at the age of eighteen and became an excellent batsman and wicketkeeper playing for England in eleven Test Matches. Throughout his first-class career he scored a total of 16,997 runs and dismissed 878 batsmen. On retirement from playing he was appointed a first-class umpire and served in this capacity in Test Matches from 1931 to 1939. In 1946 he joined the coaching staff at Edgbaston and was senior coach when Warwickshire won the Championship for the second time in 1951. Many eminent cricketers have acknowledged their indebtedness to 'Tiger' for passing on his knowledge and expertise. During the autumn of his life he was regularly to be found sitting in a corner of the players' dining-room at Edgbaston giving out advice to players as they passed by. He lived for many years in Northfield and died at his home there on 31 August 1979 at the age of ninety-three. (*A. Courbet*)

Trevor Upton with his football team from Ley Hill School in the 1960s. (*T. Upton*)

A cricket team from Longwill School. Like most schools Longwill pupils participate in a very active sports programme including football, swimming and cricket. (*Longwill School*)

Members of Worcestershire Combination & West Midland Alliance Allen's Cross Football Club who were winners of the Worcestershire Combination Cup for the 1956/7 Season. Allens Cross Football Club merged with Castle FC to be known as Cross Castle FC before adopting the name Northcross FC and then in 1966 it became Northfield Town FC. (*N. Harrison*)

Northfield Town Football Club, 1982. The club has always had a strong youth policy, which was aided by the arrival of the local Shenley Radford Youth Club in the late 1970s. Starting with two junior sides they have grown into one of the most successful youth set ups in Birmingham with ten junior football teams, and have produced outstanding top-flight footballers, such as Larry May, Colin Brazier and Eire international goalkeeper Gerry Peyton. In the 1980s Shenley Lane was granted independent status from the Allens Cross Community Association and continues to thrive to the present day. (*A. Pickering*)

Trescott School Skittle Ball Team, 1960–1. In 1960 Trescott School were playing regular skittle ball matches with away teams from other schools in the area. They all thoroughly enjoyed the games, and with Miss Morris in charge, won 75 per cent of their matches when entering for the Kings Norton Skittle Ball League. (*Trescott School*)

Miss J. Priestnall with her girls' netball team from Ley Hill School in the 1960s. Janet, who lived at 50 Church Road, recalls that around 1950 she used to visit the post office and buy £5 worth of National Savings Stamps. She would then sell them to her neighbours in Church Road, not for profit, but to help the postwar effort. Janet's grandfather, Mr Fred Crook, managed the Bournville Steam Laundry, which had a receiving office at the Northfield Institute. Her uncle, Mr Stanley Crook, ran the dry cleaning part of the business. (*J. Upton, née Priestnall*)

A swimming team from Bellfield School, the proud winners of a championship award. (*H.W.J. Green*)

Lady Morris Dancers at the Golden Jubilee celebrations at Shenley Lane Community Association and Sports Centre, June 1988. In the early 1930s Local Authorities began to build huge municipal estates on the outskirts of large cities, the two largest in Birmingham being Kingstanding and Allens Cross. The new housing was a great improvement to that from the inner city slums where most of the tenants came from, but the Local Authorities failed to provide any community or recreational facilities. The Allens Cross residents formed a Community Association to raise money to provide these facilities, a pioneering movement which, in the following twenty years was copied all over the country. With the help of George Cadbury they succeeded in building a brick hall in Tinkers Farm Road in 1931. Later Mr Christopher Cadbury and others raised sufficient money to lease twenty-two acres of land from Bournville Village Trust in Shenley Lane for use as a sports ground, comprising one cricket and two football pitches. Eventually, in 1937, work began on a clubhouse pavilion, tarmac tennis court and caretaker's house, all being officially opened on 27 August 1938 by Mr George Cadbury. (*N. Harrison*)

A ballroom dancing lesson taking place on the upper floor at Tinkers Farm School in 1952. The instructors, who received 15s per night, were Charles Depper and Margaret Lyons. Wishing to leave home Margaret saved her earnings until she had sufficient money to put a deposit on a house at Alvechurch. Jack Adkins, who was head of the Evening Institute Centre, and Margaret met there and later became husband and wife. (*M. Adkins*)

'Bluebird of Happiness' presented by the Northfield Branch of the Rutleigh-Norris School of Dancing in the George Cadbury Hall in 1984. (*V. Arthurs*)

A male voice choir, photographed in the early 1940s, which rehearsed at the Northfield Village Institute with their conductor who is believed to have been Mr Osborne. The choir sang regularly in a number of venues including Hollymoor Hospital and Winson Green Prison and won trophies in local competitions. Sydney Bowden, in the beret, came to Birmingham from Dundry, near Bristol in the early 1900s. He attended St Laurence School and later became a carpenter and joiner at the Austin Motor Works. (*D. Bowden*)

One of Trescott School's most successful choirs, which gave great enjoyment at many school concerts in 1953–4. They also participated very successfully in Northfield Music Festival, being praised for their 'Excellent effects of light and shade and good articulation, together with good contrasts, and nice diminuendos and crescendos.' They obtained 88 marks out of a possible 100, and gained First Place winning a First Class Certificate and the Stewartson Challenge Cup. In addition, in 1954, they took part in the Junior Schools' Music Festival at Birmingham Town Hall. (*Trescott School*)

St Laurence Harlequins Amateur Theatre Company performed Shows, Old Tyme Music Hall, Variety and Children's shows in the Pastoral Centre, Church Road and travelled out to organisations to entertain and raise money for charity. The Harlequins consisted of a group of over fifty keen amateurs from the age of twelve years upwards, and the money from all their productions was split between various charities. (*S. Bowden*)

A Scottish pipe band processing along the Bristol Road in the 1990s as part of the Northfield Carnival. (*R. de Boer*)

Mrs Valerie Arthurs received this photograph of the Northfield Prize Band *c.* 1910 from her uncle, Victor Hobbis, whose father played in the band. It was taken outside the Old Rectory. The conductor was the village schoolmaster, Mr Braithwaite Fewster. The band was several times the proud winner of the Annual Crystal Palace Brass Band Open Competition. (*V. Arthurs*)

Northfield Prize Band was proud winner again in 1937. Note the change of uniform. The bandmaster was Frank Wise and Dennis Frederick the Secretary. The Silver Band rehearsed in the bandroom at the Northfield Village Institute. On special occasions they would proudly lead processions around the front of the building, past Sunbury cottages, and into Victoria Common. Children assembled in their fancy dress costumes on the grassed area behind the Institute and joined the procession as it came round the corner of the building. (*P. Lewis*)

Alpha Film Group, 1950. In the 1950s Mr John Andrews, a teacher at St Laurence CE 'Old' School, made the dining-room of his house in Pamela Road into a cinema where a group of boys met regularly on a Sunday morning to watch films. They then decided to make their own films and Alpha Film Productions, comprising approximately thirty-five members between the ages of ten to twenty years, was formed. John turned a garage at the bottom of his garden into a studio and many interior and fake scenes were shot there. The studio was fully equipped with lights, and the boys were the actors who diligently rehearsed their parts. This was probably the youngest and certainly one of the most enterprising teams of amateur film makers in the locality. (*C.M. Wyeth*)

As well as interior shots the group went out on location. It became a well-established film company and produced about six films using 9.5mm film with no sound track, each film lasting approximately fifteen minutes. Each cost about 15s a minute and, by giving film shows to friends and parents, the film unit paid its way. Films made included *Village of Northfield*, *William's Television Set*, *Duet*, *World of Boys*, *End of the Chase*, *Brief Ecstasy* and *Destination Mars*. Many members of the company went on to become actors and a number trained as technicians. (*C.M. Wyeth*)

The Meadows School float at the Northfield Carnival in 1993. The school won the Carnival Float three years running. The Northfield Carnival, which raises funds for charity, opens with a procession of floats and consists of stalls, bouncy castles, children's rides and arena displays. It has been taking place each summer for many years on Victoria Common, which was given to Birmingham by George Cadbury. In 1970 there were nine hard tennis courts and two bowling greens on Victoria Common, which altogether covered approximately 21 acres. Around that time a small part of the common was taken when the Grosvenor Shopping Centre was being built, but the loss of parkland was compensated for by 4½ acres on the corner of Cob Lane, Bournville. (*The Meadows School*)

Left to right: Richard Bate, Giselia Bate, Hazel Bate, Winifred Waters, Ron Bate. Hazel and family ran a stall at Northfield Carnival for many years to collect funds for the West Midlands Swimming Club for the Disabled. Richard Bate took over as Chairman from Max Madders *c.* 1975 until the section closed through lack of funds in October 2000, after being operational for around fifty years. (*H. Bate*)

3rd Birmingham Girl Guides Company patrol leaders *c.* 1930. Jean Philips from Abbeydale Road, Barbara Hook who lived at Station House, Church Hill, and whose father was the stationmaster, and Bessie Dewar from Hawkesley Crescent. (*M. Banton*)

The launching of SRS *Silver Cloud* by Mrs W.A. Cadbury at the Manor Pool, Northfield in 1953. Mary Banton's Sea Ranger group were in the Kings Norton Division but used the Manor Pool for most of their boating activities. They were registered as SRS (Sea Ranger Ship) *Silver Cloud*. Jean Banton was 'Skipper'and Nora Barker from Heath Road 'Mate'. (*M. Banton*)

When at camp these were the daily duties to be carried out by the Girl Guides. Mary Banton, who lived in Woodland Road, Northfield was Captain of the 3rd Birmingham 1st Longbridge Estate Company, which was registered in 1923, and met in the Baptist chapel in Hawkesley Crescent. (*M. Banton*)

PATROL DUTIES

WOOD PATROL
Collect wood for Cook, Boiler and Camp fires
Chop and stack wood + cover woodpile.
Lay + light and attend to Camp Fire + Wash up for Captain.

COOK PATROL
Prepare, cook and serve meals.
Lay meals. (Each Patrol to fetch its own bags.)
Wash up cooking utensils
Wash out tea-towels.

HEALTH PATROL
Fetch drinking water from The Halts at Care of lats, wash cubicles, grease pit.
Fill boiler and light boiler fire
Wash up for Q.M.

ORDERLY PATROL
Provide Colour Party
Fetch Milk – Take Pig
Take Post – (3·30 to Mrs. Brown – The Halts)
Wait at meals + serve 2nd helpings
Care of Dining Tents, sleeping tents; keep camp site tidy and free from litter

Patrols change duties after Rest Hour each day.

Girl Guides at Redhill Camp in 1948. When the Guide country camp site at Redhill Road, Kings Norton was acquired and set up in the 1930s Mrs W.A. Cadbury, who was the County Commissioner, suggested the Pump, which was the on-site water supply, be made a meeting place for the campers similar to the Pump in villages. To achieve this, strong wooden fencing, on which the Guides could climb and sit, was built round the Pump. (*M. Banton*)

Deborah Pickvance being crowned as May Queen by Diana Collyer at Miss Alice Jones' class May Day ceremony at St Laurence CE School in 1961. (*E. Pickvance*)

This photograph was taken in 1948 of the 35th Birmingham Company Girls' Life Brigade Colour Party at Northfield Baptist Church where the brigade met. (*M. Bearman*)

The Friends' Sunday School *c.* 1953, which met at Northfield Institute where Mrs Sheila Bowden's grandfather, W.B. Parsons (of Woodyard fame), was Superintendent for fifty years. (*S. Bowden*)

Diploma awarded for one of the piano classes at Northfield Music Festival in 1954. A group of friends including Mary Dale, Nancy and Leslie Cull started Northfield Music Festival in 1950, and since its inception it has always taken place on the second Saturday in May at Turves Green Girls' School. It is a competitive festival, which began for piano, strings, school choirs and vocal classes, and later incorporated spoken word. At one point in the mid-1980s the number of spoken word entries overtook the music entries for several years, but sadly spoken word has become less popular since and the festival reverted to music classes only in 2001. It is hoped to be able to reinstate spoken word at some future date. The festival has always been run entirely by a friendly band of keen volunteers with adjudicators of high repute judging each class. Many performers have gone forward to work in the professions. (*J. Smith, née Whitehead*)

The Arms of Somery, Lords of the Manor of Northfield and Weoley.

NORTHFIELD MUSIC FESTIVAL DIPLOMA

Third

Jean Whitehead

awarded   90   marks

in the *Piano - Under 15 years* Competition

Peter Godpey   Adjudicator

19   54

"ARS GRATIA ARTIS"

May Festival, 1943. The May Festival was a yearly event, which took place between 1935 and 1959 at Tinker's Farm School. The festival centred on the investiture of a May Queen, elected by the pupils. The Queen was in her final year at school and became head girl. Each girl had a vote and the three girls obtaining the most votes became May Queen, Herald and Page. The Maids of Honour in their white and pink dresses and holding a bouquet of flowers processed on to the stage before the pageant, complete with singing, took place. Christine Read recalls her aunt from the florists Morris & Ward, making the baskets of flowers and bouquets for the May Festival. (*K.Kinneir*)

This Willow Plate Pageant was part of a Tinkers Farm May Festival. (*K.Kinneir*)

A concert performed by children from Middlemore Road. A group from this area met for various activities in 'The Hut', which was the hall belonging to St Laurence Church and built on glebe land in a field by The Darkies. It was a superior wooden building with a kitchen, toilets and stage, which was well used for various activities and performances. Dinners for children from St Laurence School were also served in 'The Hut', cooked meals being brought in. (J. Woods)

A Nativity play performed by children from Middlemore Road in 'The Hut' c. 1934–5. (J. Woods)

The play *Nordfeld to Northfield* telling the history of Northfield with libretto written by the Revd Peter Penny, and performed in the 1950s in 'The Hut'. Winifred de Boer was the Town Crier and Nancy Cull Queen Elizabeth. Mrs Edna Mann is on the front row second from the right and Mrs Margaret Leigh second from left, standing. Mrs Rawlinson, a teacher at the school, is to the left of the man in black. (*R. de Boer*)

St Laurence School play by ten-year-old children in 'The Hut', 1957. By the 1950s Roger de Boer recalls the Hut being available for St Laurence schoolchildren to eat their lunchtime sandwiches, and Mr Eastwood's woodwork classes taking place in there. (*C.M. Wyeth*)

A pageant to celebrate the 1933 Empire Day at St Laurence CE School. (*O. Williams*)

Everyone in Berwick Grove joined the street party to celebrate the Silver Jubilee of King George V and Queen Mary in 1935. (*P. Tidey-Hamilton*)

Evening celebrations round the bonfire on Church Hill on VE Day 1945. (*I. Freeman*)

John Wyeth aged eight, in patriotic suit for VE Day. Mrs Wyeth, who still lives in Pamela Road, recalls the local fishmonger in Station Road, prior to the Second World War, purchasing fish from a vendor who travelled to Northfield Station by train. She used to buy fresh sole for John when he first took solids and also recalls the fishmonger coming to their house in his pony and trap to deliver a 4*d* piece of sole when the train was late. The railway could easily be seen from their house and in about 1945 the mail train went by regularly at 9.20 each evening. John always wanted to stay up to see the train go through, so when he had been a particularly good boy he was allowed to do so. (*C.M. Wyeth*)

A street party in Pamela Road for the VE Day celebrations. Sid Taylor, who had a daughter named Pam, built the houses in Pamela Road pre-war. One day Pam Chiswell, whose parents were buying a house in the road, was splashing along the planks, which had been put down following rain to prevent people getting too muddy, when the builder asked her her name. When she told him it was Pam he decided that the road should be called Pamela Road after her and his daughter. Mrs C.M. Wyeth recalls the cost of her house in Pamela Road being £475, but they were given a £5 discount because her husband recommended a purchase in the same road to another person. (*I. Freeman*)

Everyone in Berwick Grove in party mood celebrating VE Day. (*P. Tidey-Hamilton*)

A house in Berwick Grove patriotically decorated for the coronation of Queen Elizabeth II in 1953. (*P. Tidey-Hamilton*)

A Special Coronation Open Day was held at Trescott School in May 1953 when a large number of parents and friends joined with the school in celebrating the coronation of Her Majesty, Queen Elizabeth II, in the presence of HMI Miss Hircock. The tasteful decorations in the hall were much admired, especially a model depicting the coronation of Elizabeth I, and a frieze portraying part of the present coronation procession. All classrooms were decorated in ways appropriate to the occasion, and in the playground displays of country dancing, maypole dancing and physical training were given. A programme of singing by the two school choirs and verse speaking followed. The afternoon ended with a coronation service in which visitors, children and staff participated. (*Trescott School*)

Iolanthe – the third production of Tinkers Farm Amateur Operatic Society in 1955. Tinkers Farm Amateur Operatic Society was born out of productions by boys from Tinkers Farm Secondary Modern School in the early 1950s. From these beginnings interest remained among many of the members when they left school and so the society was formed and first met on 5 February 1953 producing their first show *Devilry with the Doones* in October of that year. The society later changed its name to Tinkers Farm Opera Company and continues to produce shows to the present day. (*T. Battle*)

Northfield Amateur Operatic Society's production of *South Pacific* in 1968. St Chad's AOS produced shows at St Chad's Church Hall, Rubery, prior to 1933 when the society moved to Northfield Church Hall where productions continued until 1938. Northfield Church AOS was formed at St Laurence Church under the auspices of the Revd R.A. Haysom, who for many years took the dual role of producer and musical director. Their first production, *The Flower Queen*, was presented in May 1926 in the church hall. In 1946 it was decided to amalgamate the two societies and Northfield Operatic Society was formed. The next year, finding itself without a home, the

head of the Bournville and Northfield Evening Institute approached the society and suggested it came under the auspices of the Evening Institute, so in 1947 it met and presented its shows at Turves Green Girls' School, until the new boys' school opened in 1956 when it moved there. In 1969, for the sake of comfort for both audience and actors, the society decided to move away from Northfield to its present home at the Crescent Theatre where productions could be performed enjoying all the facilities of the professional theatre. (*S. Bowden*)

Thomas Henry Giblen, aged seventeen years. Maureen Carroll's grandfather, Thomas Henry Giblen was born on 10 December 1877 at the Naval Volunteer Inn in Bristol, of an American father and English mother. They moved to Birmingham to live in Barnsdale Crescent, Northfield, when Thomas was about four years old. He joined the Navy at Devonport on 10 December 1895 aged just twelve years, his first ship being *Impregnable*, which he joined on 11 December 1896. A copy of a page from his service record ledger states, 'All throughout his service T.H. Giblen was of very good character'. (*M. Carroll*)

In August 1907, T.H. Giblen rescued a five-year-old boy who had fallen into the canal on Monument Road, Ladywood, for which he was awarded this testimonial.

A quote from the National Roll of The Great War 1914–1918 states:–

GIBLEN, T.H. A.B. (SEAMAN GUNNER) R.N.
H.M.S. *CALYPSO*
Mobilised in August 1914 he did duty in various battleships and minesweepers during the course of hostilities, these vessels being engaged in operations in the North Sea and the Mediterranean. During his Service he acted as a Seaman Gunner and did valuable work until March 1918 when he was discharged. He holds the 1914–15 Star and the General Service and Victory Medals. (*M. Carroll*)